NATIONAL ACADEMIES
Sciences
Engineering
Medicine

NATIONAL ACADEMIES PRESS
Washington, DC

Anticipating Rare Events of Major Significance

Joe Alper and Liza Hamilton, *Rapporteurs*

Intelligence Community Studies Board

Division on Engineering and Physical Sciences

Proceedings of a Workshop

NATIONAL ACADEMIES PRESS 500 Fifth Street, NW Washington, DC 20001

This activity was supported by Contract HDTRA121P0013 with the Defense Threat Reduction Agency. Any opinions, findings, conclusions, or recommendations expressed in this publication do not necessarily reflect the views of any organization or agency that provided support for the project.

International Standard Book Number-13: 978-0-309-69306-6
International Standard Book Number-10: 0-309-69306-3
Digital Object Identifier: https://doi.org/10.17226/26698

This publication is available from the National Academies Press, 500 Fifth Street, NW, Keck 360, Washington, DC 20001; (800) 624-6242 or (202) 334-3313; http://www.nap.edu.

Copyright 2022 by the National Academy of Sciences. National Academies of Sciences, Engineering, and Medicine and National Academies Press and the graphical logos for each are all trademarks of the National Academy of Sciences. All rights reserved.

Printed in the United States of America.

Cover credit: Image courtesy of NASA's Goddard Space Flight Center.

Suggested citation: National Academies of Sciences, Engineering, and Medicine. 2022. *Anticipating Rare Events of Major Significance: Proceedings of a Workshop*. Washington, DC: The National Academies Press. https://doi.org/10.17226/26698.

The **National Academy of Sciences** was established in 1863 by an Act of Congress, signed by President Lincoln, as a private, nongovernmental institution to advise the nation on issues related to science and technology. Members are elected by their peers for outstanding contributions to research. Dr. Marcia McNutt is president.

The **National Academy of Engineering** was established in 1964 under the charter of the National Academy of Sciences to bring the practices of engineering to advising the nation. Members are elected by their peers for extraordinary contributions to engineering. Dr. John L. Anderson is president.

The **National Academy of Medicine** (formerly the Institute of Medicine) was established in 1970 under the charter of the National Academy of Sciences to advise the nation on medical and health issues. Members are elected by their peers for distinguished contributions to medicine and health. Dr. Victor J. Dzau is president.

The three Academies work together as the **National Academies of Sciences, Engineering, and Medicine** to provide independent, objective analysis and advice to the nation and conduct other activities to solve complex problems and inform public policy decisions. The National Academies also encourage education and research, recognize outstanding contributions to knowledge, and increase public understanding in matters of science, engineering, and medicine.

Learn more about the National Academies of Sciences, Engineering, and Medicine at **www.nationalacademies.org**.

Consensus Study Reports published by the National Academies of Sciences, Engineering, and Medicine document the evidence-based consensus on the study's statement of task by an authoring committee of experts. Reports typically include findings, conclusions, and recommendations based on information gathered by the committee and the committee's deliberations. Each report has been subjected to a rigorous and independent peer-review process and it represents the position of the National Academies on the statement of task.

Proceedings published by the National Academies of Sciences, Engineering, and Medicine chronicle the presentations and discussions at a workshop, symposium, or other event convened by the National Academies. The statements and opinions contained in proceedings are those of the participants and are not endorsed by other participants, the planning committee, or the National Academies.

Rapid Expert Consultations published by the National Academies of Sciences, Engineering, and Medicine are authored by subject-matter experts on narrowly focused topics that can be supported by a body of evidence. The discussions contained in rapid expert consultations are considered those of the authors and do not contain policy recommendations. Rapid expert consultations are reviewed by the institution before release.

For information about other products and activities of the National Academies, please visit www.nationalacademies.org/about/whatwedo.

PLANNING COMMITTEE ON ANTICIPATING RARE EVENTS OF MAJOR SIGNIFICANCE[1]

CHRISTOPHER L. BARRETT, University of Virginia, *Chair*
DAVID ALDOUS, NAS,[2] University of California, Berkeley
VICKI M. BIER, University of Wisconsin–Madison
DAN FUKUSHIMA, Futurist
JUSTIN C. KASPER, University of Michigan
CATO T. LAURENCIN, NAS/NAE[3]/NAM,[4] University of Connecticut Health Center
ALON ORLITSKY, University of California, San Diego
ROBERT N. SCHOCK, World Federation of Scientists
MICHELE WUCKER, Gray Rhino & Company

Staff

CARYN LESLIE, Director
DIONNA ALI, Associate Program Officer
ANTHONY FAINBERG, Senior Program Officer
LIZA HAMILTON, Senior Program Officer
MARGUERITE SCHNEIDER, Administrative Coordinator
ALAN SHAW, Director (until March 2022) and Scholar

Consultant

JOE ALPER, Consulting Writer

---

[1] The National Academies of Sciences, Engineering, and Medicine's planning committees are solely responsible for organizing the workshop, identifying topics, and choosing speakers. The responsibility for the published Proceedings of a Workshop rests with the workshop rapporteurs and the institution.
[2] Member, National Academy of Sciences.
[3] Member, National Academy of Engineering.
[4] Member, National Academy of Medicine.

INTELLIGENCE COMMUNITY STUDIES BOARD

MARK M. LOWENTHAL, Intelligence & Security Academy, LLC, *Co-Chair*
MICHAEL A. MARLETTA, NAS[1]/NAM,[2] University of California, Berkeley, *Co-Chair*
JOEL F. BRENNER, Massachusetts Institute of Technology
ROBERT T. CARDILLO, The Cardillo Group, LLC
FREDERICK R. CHANG, NAE,[3] Southern Methodist University
DEAN B. CHENG, The Heritage Foundation
ROBERT DYNES, NAS, University of California, San Diego
ROBERT A. FEIN, McLean Hospital/Harvard Medical School
HUBAN A. GOWADIA, Lawrence Livermore National Laboratory
MIRIAM E. JOHN, Independent Consultant
ANITA K. JONES, NAE, University of Virginia
STEVEN E. KOONIN, NAS, New York University
CARMEN L. MIDDLETON, The Walt Disney Company
ARTHUR L. MONEY, NAE, Independent Consultant
WILLIAM C. OSTENDORFF, United States Naval Academy
DAVID A. RELMAN, NAM, Stanford University
ELIZABETH RINDSKOPF PARKER, Retired, State Bar of California
SAMUEL S. VISNER, The MITRE Corporation
DAVID A. WHELAN, NAE, University of California, San Diego

Staff

CARYN LESLIE, Director
DIONNA ALI, Associate Program Officer
BRYAN FROST BUNNELL, Research Associate
ANTHONY FAINBERG, Senior Program Officer
NIA JOHNSON, Program Officer
CHRIS JONES, Senior Finance Business Partner
MARGUERITE SCHNEIDER, Administrative Coordinator

---

[1] Member, National Academy of Sciences.
[2] Member, National Academy of Medicine.
[3] Member, National Academy of Engineering.

Reviewers

This Proceedings of a Workshop was reviewed in draft form by individuals chosen for their diverse perspectives and technical expertise. The purpose of this independent review is to provide candid and critical comments that will assist the National Academies of Sciences, Engineering, and Medicine in making each published proceedings as sound as possible and to ensure that it meets the institutional standards for quality, objectivity, evidence, and responsiveness to the charge. The review comments and draft manuscript remain confidential to protect the integrity of the process.

We thank the following individuals for their review of this proceedings:

Vicki M. Bier, University of Wisconsin–Madison,
Terik Daly, Johns Hopkins University Applied Physics Laboratory, and
Seth Guikema, University of Michigan.

Although the reviewers listed above provided many constructive comments and suggestions, they were not asked to endorse the content of the proceedings nor did they see the final draft before its release. The review of this proceedings was overseen by Thomas J. Overby, NAE,[1] Texas A&M University. He was responsible for making certain that an independent examination of this proceedings was carried out in accordance with standards of the National Academies and that all review comments were carefully considered. Responsibility for the final content rests entirely with the rapporteurs and the National Academies.

---

[1] Member, National Academy of Engineering.

Contents

1	INTRODUCTION AND OVERVIEW	1
2	MATHEMATICAL FOUNDATIONS FOR ANTICIPATING RARE EVENTS	3
3	DETECTION, INDICATIONS, AND WARNINGS	5
	Heading Off Megafires with Artificial Intelligence, 5	
	Experiences with Anticipatory Analytics and Rare Events, 6	
	Risks, Warnings, and Signals: A Systems/Risk Analysis Perspective, 7	
	Discussion, 9	
4	PLANNING, FORECASTING, AND INTELLIGENCE PREPARATION	11
	Down to Earth with an Electric Hazard from Space, 11	
	Planning for Rare Events: Supporting Good Governance for Resilience, 13	
	Planning and Responding to Significant Rare Events, 14	
	Discussion, 15	
5	FIRESIDE CHAT—USING ARTIFICIAL INTELLIGENCE TO PREDICT THE OCCURRENCE OF SEPSIS	17
6	FIRESIDE CHAT—RARE EVENTS AND INSURANCE	20
7	MULTISOURCE INFORMATION FUSION, SITUATION ASSESSMENT, AND COURSE OF ACTION SELECTION	23
	Overcoming Failures of Imagination, 23	
	Severe Space Weather as a Source of Rare Events of Major Significance, 25	
	Experiences from Black Sky Planning, 26	
	Discussion, 28	

8 ACTIVE PREVENTION AND DETERRENCE 30
   Asteroid Impacts—Thinking About an Uncertain Threat, 30
   The Challenges of Addressing Rare Events and How to Overcome Them, 32
   Dealing with Extremes in Economics and Finance, 34
   Discussion, 36

9 CONCLUDING REMARKS 38

APPENDIXES

A Statement of Task 43
B Workshop Agenda 44
C Planning Committee Biographies 47
D Speaker Biographies 50

1

Introduction and Overview

The Intelligence Community Studies Board (ICSB) of the National Academies of Sciences, Engineering, and Medicine convened a 2-day virtual workshop on December 17 and 21, 2021, to explore insights from world-class experts and technologists familiar with the extensive range of issues associated with anticipating rare events—those characterized by a very low probability of occurring—of major significance.

Intelligence preparation of the battlefield includes information about, and warnings related to, significant rare events.

Intelligence preparation for high-risk environments catalyzed by rare events requires some of the most difficult types of time-sensitive data collection, situational interpretation, and analysis to establish priorities using multiple criteria. Developing decision advantage through the analysis of rare events requires the consideration of both qualitative and quantitative factors, such as the possibility of the event, the elements and circumstances of the event as it occurs, and the consequences of the event.

Because rare event analysis is often plagued by data sparsity, noise, ambiguity, and contextual bias from data sources, it is not always possible to properly align opportunistic sets of data about a rare event gathered separately and independently across various contexts. Additionally, because the data often are collected opportunistically and not in a focused way, it can be incomplete or of poor quality for this purpose. Taken together, these factors can result in reliance on interpretive operations that push the limits of purely data-driven analysis and lead to vulnerability to deception or bias-related misinterpretation. Conversely, the use of highly focused, specific, rare event–directed sensing and data collection resources intended to increase sensitivity can increase the probability for missed signals and false alarms. In the case of operational environments, a rare event would be characterized by any extreme disruption of routine objectives, context, and other characteristics of those operations and environment.

In summary, data collected about an unpredicted event can range from being opportunistic, contextually constrained, and relatively uncontrolled to highly focused and specific. In either case, some data about the event, possibly more generally useful, could easily go unmeasured or remain unknown, given the particular operational context. Thus it might be difficult to align specific operational data about a rare event with other data collected for other purposes about that particular or similar event. Correlations can become tenuous, entirely illusory, or even become lost.

The U.S. Defense Threat Reduction Agency (DTRA)-sponsored workshop (see Appendix A for the original statement of task) described in the upcoming chapters was forged out of the need for greater focus on rare events. In turn, this workshop also called for greater institutional consideration and incorporation of the way rare event data are both collected and analyzed.

Over the course of the 2-day workshop, the speakers discussed analytical methods, computational advances, data sources, and risk assessment approaches for anticipating rare events, including natural disasters, pandemics, anthropogenic threats, and widespread technological change.

Christopher Barrett, chair of the planning committee, opened the workshop by noting that the idea of anticipating rare events of major significance immediately raises a variety of complicated issues, such as how to know something is major, how to look for it when it has never happened before, or how to know which of the many minor events that occur will emerge and become significant. Each of these vexing issues is begging for better solutions. He also mentioned the challenge of assigning responsibility to individuals, organizations, and even artificial intelligence systems for making judgments and interpreting situations as they pertain to anticipating and preparing for a rare event of major significance. He then introduced Theodore Plasse, chief of the Analysis and Plans Division at DTRA, to provide background and perspective from the sponsor.

Plasse explained that the Department of Defense (DoD) created DTRA in 1998 to provide better predictive analysis that would enable actions to counter weapons of mass destruction (WMDs). His team started with a predictive analysis that forecasts enemy courses of action based on space and time, geographic positions, where things move around, how long they take to move, and when they will come together. With some reworking of this general model, the team was successful at satisfying the task it was given, and it has since worked with the Intelligence Advanced Research Projects Activity (IARPA) to further refine this model for conducting predictive analysis for WMD. This workshop came about, said Plasse, after he attended ICSB meetings and spoke with its members about the possibility of expanding DTRA's work beyond WMD.

To conduct this workshop, ICSB appointed a workshop planning committee to identify potential speakers and design the workshop agenda. Planning committee members and National Academies staff worked with the sponsor in advance of the meeting to refine the workshop's topics for discussion. Approximately 85 participants, including the planning committee, invited panelists, national security community staff and officials, and National Academies staff, participated in the virtual workshop.

The workshop rapporteurs prepared this proceedings as a factual summary of what occurred at the workshop. The planning committee's role was limited to planning the workshop. Statements, recommendations, and opinions expressed are those of individual presenters and participants, and are not necessarily endorsed or verified by the National Academies, and they should not be construed as reflecting any group consensus.

2

Mathematical Foundations for Anticipating Rare Events

To begin his presentation, Alon Orlitsky, professor of electrical and computer engineering at the University of California, San Diego, noted that when two legendary researchers—Martin Helmut, who co-developed public key cryptography, and Vinton Cerf, who designed one of the first Internet protocols—argued in a recent paper[1] about the probability of having a nuclear war in the following year, the only thing they could agree on was that the risk was too high. The fact that these two prominent thinkers could not even agree on whether there was a probability for this event, let alone what that probability is, suggests that the problem is unsolvable and that there is no mathematical solution for the probability that there will be a nuclear incident in the following year.

Rather than talk about the probability of nuclear war, Orlitsky said his presentation would focus on topics where it is possible to derive rigorous, mathematically provable results about rare and unseen events. The difference between a nuclear event and a solvable rare event is that the former is a binary event—it either does or does not happen—for which Orlitsky argues prediction is impossible. This is not just theory, he said, but something that is done frequently. Examples of what are known as "large domain problems" include machine translation and transcription, which involve predicting which rare word might come next in a sentence, and predicting where a terrorist attack might occur, given the many possible cities where an attack might occur and the many different terrorist groups that could launch an attack.

The first notable success at solving a large domain problem came during World War II, when I.J. Good and Alan Turing were trying to decipher the German enigma code. This effort involved trying to guess the approximate location of a password taken from a large book. In this case, each word in the book has a very low probability of being chosen, making it a rare event. The two mathematicians developed an estimation formula, known as the Good-Turing formula that even today is used in many applications, including speech recognition. This formula calculates the probability of rare events and unseen events when there are a large number of elements involved, such as predicting what the next word in a sentence will be given the large number of words in the English language and the frequency with which they occur in other sentences. Orlitsky and his students have used the Good-Turing formula to see if they could predict the number of terrorist incidents in different types of cities in the next year given the number of terrorist incidents in the current year. For data, they used the National Consortium for the Study of Terrorism and Responses to Terrorism (START) global terrorism database[2] of more than 50,000 events

---

[1] M.E. Hellman and V.G. Cerf, 2021, "An Existential Discussion: What *Is* the Probability of Nuclear War?," *Bulletin of the Atomic Scientists*, March 18, 2021, https://thebulletin.org/2021/03/an-existential-discussion-what-is-the-probability-of-nuclear-war.

[2] See the START global terrorism database at https://www.start.umd.edu/gtd, last updated May 2022.

in some 12,000 cities from 1992 to 2010, and they based their predictions for cities where no events or few events occurred in a given year on data from the previous year. The results, said Orlitsky, tracked well with the actual number of terrorist events that occurred in those cities.

Orlitsky then discussed methods for estimating the probabilities of multiple events simultaneously and probabilities over future time periods based on observations in a previous time period. By analogy, after observing the number of words in the first 10 percent of Shakespeare's *Hamlet*, one could estimate the number of different words in the remainder of the play. He also described methods for estimating the probabilities of events occurring when the data come from many sources, some of which are likely to be wrong.

David Aldous, a member of the planning committee, commented that the methods Orlitsky discussed treat data as if they do not have any structure. As an example, he noted that the cities where terrorist attacks occur have a structure that would be good to include in calculating those probabilities. Similarly, Barrett noted that because systems are not stable and are constantly evolving, it will be necessary to perform these calculations repeatedly as the underlying estimates change. Orlitsky added that there are instances involving competition where these approaches do not work.

3

Detection, Indications, and Warnings

The workshop's first panel session featured three presentations addressing different approaches to spotting rare events in their nascent stage. The three speakers were Arvind Satyam, chief commercial officer at Pano AI; T. Charles Clancy, senior vice president, general manager of MITRE Labs, and chief futurist at MITRE; and Elisabeth Paté-Cornell, the Burt and Deedee McMurtry Professor and founding chair of the Department of Management Science and Engineering at Stanford University. Robert Schock, senior fellow at the Center for Global Security Research at Lawrence Livermore National Laboratory and planning committee member, moderated a discussion following the presentations.

HEADING OFF MEGAFIRES WITH ARTIFICIAL INTELLIGENCE

When Arvind Satyam and his colleagues at Pano AI thought about how they could apply artificial intelligence (AI) to the problem of protecting physical spaces and infrastructure from wildfires, they realized that the number of wildfires had not increased dramatically, but the number of megafires has, as a result of hotter, dryer weather, extended for longer periods of time. California, for example, has had six of the ten largest fires in the state's history occur since August 2020. He noted that researchers studying places like California and the east coast of Australia, where megafires have become a huge problem, have concluded that the single biggest determinant of whether a fire will turn into a large incident is how quickly it is spotted and confirmed and how quickly local fire officials mount a response. It was this realization, he said, that led him and his colleagues to focus on detecting fires when they are small so they could provide actionable intelligence to end users, including fire authorities; emergency response systems; city, state, and federal response agencies; utility companies; and insurance firms.

Today, most incidents come to the attention of fire officials thanks to people calling emergency phone lines, and while those alerts are valuable, they rarely include precise locations that can shave critical minutes off the all-important initial response. Pano AI's approach was to deploy pairs of ultrahigh-definition rotating cameras and use software to simulate the experience of a person sitting on a traditional fire watchtower. The result is an AI system that analyzes the continuously rotating image to spot texture, movement, and gradients in the images indicative of the smoke plume emitted by even the smallest fire. Training the AI enables it to distinguish between smoke and clouds, even on hazy days, and to do so for different terrains.

Pano AI has deployed this system in California, Colorado, Montana, and Oregon—Australia is on tap to deploy the system in the beginning of 2022[1]—and the AI learns from each of these different environments. California alone, for example, has more than 20 microclimates from which AI training can occur. At the time of the workshop, the AI data set contained more than 300 million images, and Satyam said the system's performance continues to improve as that data set grows. To deal with potential false positives, the company has a fully staffed intelligence center with a team of analysts who can review prior footage to aid in quickly determining if a detection is a true incident.

Satyam pointed out that the multiple camera placements in each location allow the system to triangulate and pinpoint the exact location of the fire. This not only aids the local fire authority, but it enables the local utility to understand where the incident is relative to its transmission lines and enables insurance companies to know where the incident is relative to its insured assets. He added that an optical zoom feature allows local fire officials to actually see flames connected to a smoke detection more than 10 miles from a camera, which lets them determine how to coordinate a response, such as calling in an aerial attack.

On a final note, Satyam said the system can now pull in data from the GOES-16 and GOES-17 weather satellites, and it can also access feeds from other cameras that happen to be in the deployed environments. One goal, he said, is to overlay more infrastructure assets to provide better information for end users.

EXPERIENCES WITH ANTICIPATORY ANALYTICS AND RARE EVENTS

Charles Clancy explained that his projects with IARPA aimed to leverage emerging big data capabilities and advances in AI and machine learning to develop anticipatory analytics for predicting the next war and forecasting events such as a terrorist attack, social unrest, and local election outcomes. The initial effort focused on social media and expanded to include cyber threat data and classified government data.

Clancy explained that a system, which emerged from this work, used time-referenced data from a wide variety of sources, such as the velocity of a particular hashtag on social media, to extract features that would then feed into models that generated the relevant forecasts. The idea was to build models based on the available data and let the system determine which models are generating useful output and which are generating less useful output. Each model creates several candidate forecasted events that feed into a fusion engine, which identifies duplicate forecasts and either suppresses or advances certain forecasts based on quality metrics. The system builds these quality metrics over time from the various models providing the data.

A key feature of the system is that a person hand codes actual ground truths of events that have happened in the targeted class of events and in the targeted region of the world. The coding includes the type, severity, time, and location of these real-world events. The system then learns by comparing forecasted to actual events, accounting for noise. For example, the forecasted event might be off by a day, its location might be off by a few miles, or the severity might have been different. The results of these comparisons go into a scoring system that assesses forecast accuracy and lead time. The goal is to forecast an event days or even a week or more in advance.

The first conclusion from this work, Clancy observed, is that models that rely exclusively on the time-delayed ground truth—so-called base rate models—work well. As a theoretical example, if the goal is to know how many protests are going to happen in Mexico City in a particular month, the easiest thing to predict there will be the same number as happened in the previous month. In essence, the base rate models make sophisticated guesses based on probability distributions.

Typically, Clancy was attempting to use these models to forecast the number of events that would happen during 1 month with a resolution[2] of 1 day. Improving the forecasts involved determining how to leverage big data to modulate up or down the number of events in a particular class that would occur over the next month. "The unsatisfying part of this is once you have the number of events you expect the next month, you just randomly

---

[1] Pano AI, 2020, "Pano AI's Early Bushfire Detection Technology Gives Southern Cross Forests More Tools to Prevent Bushfires in New South Wales," release date March 8, 2020, https://newsdirect.com/news/pano-ais-early-bushfire-detection-technology-gives-southern-cross-forests-more-tools-to-prevent-bushfires-in-new-south-wales-353650975.

[2] The reporting resolution of 1 day means time was quantized in to 24-hour periods. Event times were reported as dates, but not dates and times.

generate your forecasts to equal that total, subject to the a priori distribution that you have from your base rate model," Clancy noted.

As a result, he became concerned that intelligence agencies would be using this system to make actual intelligence assessments and forecast events when the created forecasts were, for the most part, randomly generated according to a probability distribution. The problem is that if the models generate enough events, the matching algorithm will say that most of them are close to an actual event as long as the total number was correct. Clancy observed, "This worked well for predicting any sort of event that had sufficient volume for the law of large numbers to kick in, but if you did not have enough volume of events, this thing works terribly." In other words, Clancy explained, this approach does not work well for rare events in a meaningful time frame, although it might be able to generate a forecast that 37 years from now, plus or minus 5 years, China will invade Taiwan, to cite a possibility at random.

To handle rare events, Clancy created a separate set of models designed by human experts with subject-matter expertise. These models use "small data" and inject their forecasts into the AI system, but this approach performed no better than having a human executing the same task. This approach, he noted, helped automate some of the processes, but it did not have the ability to piece together disparate facts from multiple data sets in a way that could outperform humans. A lesson for the Intelligence Community is that it is important to get the analysts with subject-matter expertise involved in the development and execution of these projects, because using this type of volumetric approach will not work for rare event forecasting.

In terms of research opportunities going forward, Clancy suggested that advances in AI and machine learning have created more sophisticated approaches for generating synthetic data through generative adversarial networks. Reinforcement learning is also dramatically improving the ability to create agents that can detect events. Toward that end, he is creating synthetic, big data sets with a rare event buried in them to train algorithms to find that event. He also noted the challenge of capturing analyst expertise at scale, which the AI community is tackling by designing algorithms to work with humans rather than assuming that the AI algorithm will arrive at a useful answer by itself. The goal is to make AI part of the analyst team and help the analysts be more efficient in applying their subject-matter expertise to a problem.

Clancy mentioned the large gap in the ability of AI to do contextual and causal reasoning that would enable AI to tackle the small data problem. Some in the AI community have suggested using AI to detect anomalies, but the problem is that an analyst still needs to look at the anomaly to determine whether it is a false positive. Cybersecurity uses this approach, but it generates so many false positives that analysts do not find them useful because it creates too many leads for them to examine. He added that anomaly detection is not likely to be useful for rare events because of the large number of anomalies that occur every day.

RISKS, WARNINGS, AND SIGNALS: A SYSTEMS/RISK ANALYSIS PERSPECTIVE

Elisabeth Paté-Cornell began her presentation by discussing a general model for optimizing a warning threshold so that it does not give too many false positives or false negatives. This stochastic model includes a warning threshold, which generates alerts (true or false), and a critical threshold, above which there is real trouble. Two other components of this model are (1) the effect of memory on response to signals, which occurs when people remember the accuracy of the last alert(s) and (2) the lead time provided. That lead time is the time elapsed between the time when the signal appears because the hazard level has crossed the warning threshold, and the time when the hazard level crosses the critical threshold. If the warning threshold is set too high, the lead time will be short, although there will be fewer false alerts. If it is set too low, there will be more time to respond, but more false alerts.

Optimizing a warning system thus involves balancing the trade-offs among the up-crossing rate of the stochastic process, the memory effects, and the length and use of the lead time, explained Paté-Cornell. The process for doing so is to model first the stochastic process of the system's evolution (e.g., how the water in a river goes up and down), then to assess the up-crossing rates associated with possible alert thresholds. The next step involves analyzing people's responses to a warning signal, given what they remember of the accuracy of past warnings and the benefits of the lead time that the signals provide. One can then determine the optimal level of an alert by balancing the trade-off between Type 1 and Type 2 errors (false positives and false negatives). The final step is to determine the value of the information provided by a warning system in terms of people's responses and decisions in the face of a hazard.

Paté-Cornell's first of two examples of how such a model can produce useful warnings involved monitoring satellites in low Earth orbit to avoid collisions with debris, based on the Ph.D. thesis of Richard Kim[3] under her supervision. She compared two monitoring systems of different cost and reliability. The U.S. Space Surveillance Network uses more than 20 ground-based optical systems and radars, along with several orbiting satellites, and is considered the more sensitive. The international scientific optical network uses a larger number of telescopes around the world but is less accurate. Together, the two systems send information to satellite operators, who then make tactical decisions about moving a satellite, given a warning signal to avoid a collision.

The issue Paté-Cornell and her co-author explored was to determine which strategic option was better for improving the warning system. As an illustration, they compared the options to spend $100 million to add one sensor to the U.S. Space Surveillance Network or to add 35 sensors to the international optical network at the same cost. To answer that question, they used a Bayesian framework to update the probability of a threat, given the complex message coming from the two systems and the probability of failing to issue a timely alert. Based on the illustrative values that they used to describe the behavior of users, and given the information that they may receive from these networks, it turns out that adding 35 small sensors to the international optical network would provide information that is worth more than the information gained by adding one large sensor to the U.S. Space Surveillance Network.

"This Bayesian framework helps support rational decisions, both tactical and strategic," said Paté-Cornell, "The value of the monitoring system is based on the costs of the failure risks, and the model provides a basis for comparing two monitoring systems with different capabilities." She cautioned that their quantitative inputs were merely illustrative and that these results should not be used for making decisions.

The objective of the second example, based on the thesis of Isaac Faber[4] under her supervision, was to anticipate and prevent catastrophic cyber-attacks by generating early warnings of cyber threats using a hybrid system involving AI and a human operator. The response to a warning signal involves a trade-off between the risk of stopping a legitimate entry and the benefits of preventing an attack—for instance, to protect a hospital's system from cyber threats.

There are two broad categories of actors, Paté-Cornell explained, those with legitimate access and those with malicious intent who are attempting to pass through a series of cybersecurity gates to reach critical files. These gates are the steps in the sequence of operations that need to be successful for the attack to actually occur (the "kill chain"). The challenge is to develop a gate policy that optimizes the trade-off between blocking threats and allowing legitimate access. The questions are, When should the computer act alone? and When should the human operator intervene? Both the computer and the human expert have access to (imperfect) information from the main stack, which is continuously updated by external information and by experience with various actors. When the system first starts operating on a problem, the human expert makes many of the decisions on whether to open or close a gate, because at that point, the AI system, although it may have access to a lot of information, does not have enough knowledge to process all new signals. Over time, though, the AI learns how to do this, but it can also decide to pass the hand to the human operator when it recognizes that the uncertainties or the possible outcomes are too large.

To train the system, Paté-Cornell and her co-author put 18 honeypots[5] around the world and got about 600,000 visits to those honeypots. Some came from unique Internet Protocol (IP) addresses, some were on blacklists, and nearly 12,000 had multiple entries. The warning system used the frequencies of those attacks to identify threats. Most of the blacklisted events came from China, with the United States, France, and Russia also accounting for a significant number of the threats. She noted that the honeypots generated a database that issued signals to the

---

[3] R.H. Kim, 2018, "Managing the Risk of Satellite Collisions: A Probabilistic Risk Analysis of Improving Space Surveillance Systems," Ph.D. thesis, Stanford University, Stanford, CA, http://purl.stanford.edu/rx304kb4324.

[4] I.J. Faber, 2019. "Cyber Risk Management: AI-Generated Warnings of Threats," Ph.D. thesis, Stanford University, Stanford, CA, https://purl.stanford.edu/mw190gm2975.

[5] A "honeypot" is a cybersecurity mechanism that uses a manufactured attack target to lure cybercriminals away from legitimate targets. They also gather intelligence about the identity, methods, and motivations of adversaries.

defenders about the attackers and sometimes to the attackers about the defenders as well. The raw data from the honeypots were used to update the central database of IP addresses, along with the probability that each entry was from an attacker. Both the AI system and the human agent then used the updated central database to decide which gates to open next.

One takeaway from this example, said Paté-Cornell, is that one can use observed behaviors (along with external information) as signals of threats to inform the decision of the hybrid AI–human cybersecurity system to open or close a gate in a computer system.

She noted that warnings can be qualitatively interpreted, but that quantification with probabilities helps with interpreting warnings and comparing options. This is particularly true when the warning messages are complex, as was the case of satellite monitoring by two systems. She also pointed out that an AI and human hybrid system is helpful when using a database that evolves constantly and when making quick decisions is critical when dealing with attackers who move fast.

DISCUSSION

All three speakers noted the importance of continually updating the database that powers an AI system to reflect new or changing underlying conditions or a better understanding of the factors that can influence the underlying conditions. Satyam pointed out how important this was for the fire detection system because it is deployed in different environments.

When asked how she measures the precision of the AI and human in her system, Paté-Cornell observed that the problems that the system addresses deal with uncertainties, and that the best information to describe them is the probability distributions of the factors involved. These distributions of probability allow rational decisions without pretending that there is a known "precise" (certain) value to the factors involved. The objective is thus to represent these uncertainties as well as possible to support critical decisions.

Nestor Alfonzo Santamaria from the Organisation for Economic Co-operation and Development (OECD) asked Clancy and Paté-Cornell how they escape the trap of giving false confidence in results that have high uncertainty. Clancy replied that models can provide confidence intervals associated with their forecasts and provide the provenance of the underlying data used to produce a forecast. The systems he has built, for example, would provide traceability back to the underlying social media messages that led to deriving a particular conclusion. Analysts could then make their own judgment about whether to agree with the forecast. Santamaria said that approach is sufficient when the analysts are experienced, but he talks to policy makers who are not experts in the field, to which Clancy replied that he has not seen a forecasting system that should be producing policy recommendations. Paté-Cornell added that her goal is to represent uncertainties as best as she can and to inform the decision maker about those uncertainties. It is then up to the decision makers to decide how much risk they are willing to take, based on imperfect information.

Satyam noted that this issue is why it is important to spend time coupling human intelligence on top of information produced by AI and of creating a virtuous loop that ends up producing more accurate results than either AI or human would produce on their own. Christopher Barrett added that in a changing environment, the goal is to build a cohesive, integrated representation of a system that can convey meaningful information to the decision process. The goal is not to generate precise, predictive outcomes.

Both Clancy and Barrett pointed to the challenge of dealing with a system where the data come in so slowly that by the time a system can use that data to make a prediction, the prediction is no longer relevant. One project Clancy worked on involved an emergency department clinician typing into the search box of the electronic health record to find the diagnostic code used to denote that a patient had COVID-19. This real-time data provided a week or two lead time on the typical data that enabled him to improve the fidelity and timeliness of the actionable output that decision makers could use. Both Clancy and Paté-Cornell noted there is often a trade-off between the speed of a response based on less-than-perfect information and what that response would be if there was more time to gather information.

Schock asked the panelists to forecast where the forecasting field will be in 5–10 years. Paté-Cornell replied that she believes there will be progress in how AI systems process information and their ability to make automated decisions. Satyam noted that as climate change produces more extreme weather events, there will be richer data sets with which to train Pano AI's systems, and it will be able to integrate more data feeds that will be polling in real time. Clancy expressed his hope that national security events will not increase to the point that there will be more good training data for these models. The synthetic models will improve, though, simply because there will be more computational power available, as well as better detectors that are better grounded in reality.

Jeffrey J. Love from the U.S. Geological Survey (USGS) pointed to the need to test and validate models designed to predict rare events. For that reason, he wonders about the value of models for predicting the future likelihood of nuclear war, since those models cannot be validated. What they might be useful for, Love pointed out, could be to help provide insights into various concepts that might lead to a nuclear event. Along the same lines, David Sweeney from DTRA asked how to train models where there is either no training data or insufficient ground truths. Theodore Plasse, DTRA, interjected that the goal is not to predict when nuclear war might happen. Instead, the goal is to mine data about the equipment and processes that go into making a nuclear bomb to inform a system that could generate predictions about who is trying to make a bomb, the precursor event to the event.

Getting back to Sweeney's question, Clancy said using synthetic data is one possibility to addressing the unavailability of training data or ground truths. Another potential approach is transfer learning, which involves training the AI on data from an adjacent field and then revising the model using the small amount of data in a new field. He noted that there is a growing number of successes using this approach. A third tactic is to leverage other facets of AI, such as inference and reasoning that are well-developed fields that capitalize on applying analyst expertise to the problem.

4

Planning, Forecasting, and Intelligence Preparation

The workshop's second panel session featured presentations on the analysis and forecasting aspects of preparing intelligence and decision support products for end users such as DTRA. The three speakers were Jeffrey J. Love, USGS's adviser for geomagnetic research and a member of the Space Weather Operations Research and Mitigation Working Group of the National Science and Technology Council; Nestor Alfonzo Santamaria, senior adviser on risk governance at OECD; and Madhav Marathe, distinguished professor in biocomplexity at the University of Virginia Biocomplexity Institute. Christopher Barrett moderated the discussion following the three presentations.

DOWN TO EARTH WITH AN ELECTRIC HAZARD FROM SPACE

Earth's core, said Love, is a naturally occurring electric current generator, which in turn produces magnetic fields that thread their way out of the core, through Earth's mantle, up to Earth's surface, and out into space. The extent to which the magnetic field expands into space defines the magnetosphere. When the magnetosphere interacts with electrically charged particles in the solar wind, it induces electric currents in Earth's interior. Because systems such as power grids are grounded to the earth, they pick up these naturally occurring, changing, electric fields, which in turn can cause problems.

Space weather, Love continued, results when the Sun gives off an occasional coronal burst of plasma, which a couple of days later arrives at Earth and compresses its magnetosphere on the daylight side and extends it on the nighttime side. The rearrangement of the magnetic lines within the magnetosphere produces currents that travel into and out of Earth's ionosphere, generating the beautiful aurora borealis and, also, possibly causing disruptions to critical infrastructure. One such magnetic storm in September 1859, often described as the most intense magnetic storm in recorded history, caused widespread disruption of telegraphic services. Another notable magnetic storm in May 1921 disrupted radio, telegraph, and telephone communications and triggered at least three fires in New York railway stations. A March 1940 solar storm caused widespread disruption of long-wire communication systems, and storms in May 1967 and August 1972 interfered with military operations.

The most recent major magnetic storm, March 1989, caused the complete collapse of the Canadian Hydro-Quebec power system, about $3 billion to $6 billion Canadian dollars in damage in Canada, electrical blackouts in Sweden, interference to the U.S. electrical grid, damage to a high-voltage transformer in New Jersey, disruption of geophysical surveys, and damage to orbiting satellites. Given this history and society's dependence on electrical technology, Love posed a critical question, What would the effect on modern society be if there was a recurrence of the 1859 or 1921 magnetic storms?

In fact, the National Academies issued a workshop report on that very subject in 2008.[1] That workshop report noted that a magnetic super storm could cause significant damage to and interference with military satellites; widespread disruption of GPSs, radio communication, and geophysical surveys; widespread and prolonged loss of electricity resulting from damage to the electric grid; and a possible economic impact to the United States of $1 trillion to $2 trillion. The challenge in accurately predicting the effects of such a storm is that, even though magnetic super storms have occurred in the past, society is now, more than ever, dependent on technology that is vulnerable to magnetic storms. Love explained that the possible occurrence of such a storm led to the establishment of the Space Weather Operations Research and Mitigation Working Group within the White House National Science and Technology Council to coordinate activities among federal agencies concerned about space weather.

Statistical modeling has produced estimates that a magnetic storm such as the one that occurred in 1989 will occur every 44 years or so. At the same time, while the 1859 or 1921 storms appear to be 500-year events,[2] there have been two significant storms since 1859. This, observed Love, highlights one of the challenges of retrospective statistical analyses of rare events. He added that describing the intensity or size of a rare event, such as a massive magnetic storm with a single number, is almost always simplistic, in part because such an extreme storm transpires in complex ways over a period of time. Magnetic storms typically last several days, which means that the scalars one might hope to use in standard statistical analyses do not describe these events well. Some phenomena, Love described, change over long time scales, introducing non-stationarity, which is a problem in many statistical analyses.

Turning to the March 1989 magnetic storm, Love described the physics involved when a magnetic storm damages a high-voltage transformer. The key feature here is that Earth's structure is heterogeneous, with some regions being good electrical conductors as a result of their particular mineralogy and fluid content, while other regions are more resistant. As a result, the electric field generated by a magnetic storm will not be as effective at driving currents in some regions of Earth compared to other regions. If a power grid spans an electrically resistive region, the electric current will take the path of least resistance, which would be to flow through the power grid rather than the earth. The current would flow into and out of the earth through ground connections, which typically occur at transformer stations. The power grid is not designed to accommodate such "quasi-direct" currents, which is why they damage transformers.[3] "This is the crux of the problem for the power grid industry in terms of space weather," deduced Love.

To map geoelectric hazards across the United States, Love and his collaborators have adopted an empirical model approach familiar from time series analysis:

- An input signal that varies over time—the geomagnetic variation generated by the Sun,
- Convolution of that signal through a filter—Earth's heterogeneous composition, and
- An output signal that varies over time—a geoelectric field that can damage power grids.

Powering the model are magnetic observatory data that record geomagnetic variation at stations across the United States and Canada and survey data from magnetotelluric measurements that yield Earth's surface impedance as a function of location. Love noted that the magnetotelluric survey is an ongoing project, with much of Arizona, Texas, Oklahoma, Arkansas, Louisiana, and Mississippi. Parts of Utah, Kansas, and Alabama have yet to be surveyed. The existing survey, which presently covers two-thirds of the contiguous United States, shows high impedance in the upper Midwest and Eastern United States, with low impedance in Michigan, Illinois, the Appalachian basin, and much of the western United States.

---

[1] National Research Council, 2008, *Severe Space Weather Events: Understanding Societal and Economic Impacts: A Workshop Report*, The National Academies Press, Washington, DC.

[2] That is, events assessed as expected to occur at this frequency.

[3] J.J. Love, E.J. Rigler, A. Pulkkinen, and C.C. Balch, 2014, "Magnetic Storms and Induction Hazards," *Eos, Transactions, American Geophysical Union* 95(48):445–446, https://doi.org/10.1002/2014EO480001.

Using these inputs, the modeling method used by Love and his collaborators provides geoelectric field estimates that can then be mapped onto power grids to estimate line voltages. The method was used to estimate the maximum geoelectric fields experienced during the March 1989 storm. That storm, according to the model, would have produced high electric field amplitudes of two to three orders of greater magnitude in the upper Midwest and along the Eastern Seaboard than in other places, such as in Michigan or across most of the western United States. High geoelectric amplitude correlates with the reported interference that power grids experienced during the 1989 storm. This geoelectric hazard analysis, combined with the March 1989 record of anomalies in the power grid, suggests that the U.S. Mid-Atlantic and Northeast regions are where high geoelectric hazards are likely to be experienced during an even more intense storm.

Presently, Love and his collaborators are working with the National Oceanic and Atmospheric Administration (NOAA) to create real-time geoelectric hazard maps. Such maps, he explained, would be useful for nowcasting, an important tool for managing the power grid system during an intense magnetic storm. In addition, the USGS team has developed a statistical map of geoelectric hazards, such as would be experienced by a 100-year magnetic storm on voltages the national power grid would experience and indicates where the hazards of damage are high and low.

An offshoot of this project, said Love, is that it also provides information as to where the nation might concentrate its efforts to understand the hazards of an E3 nuclear electromagnetic pulse (EMP). Such a pulse, which would last tens to hundreds of seconds, results from a nuclear explosion's distortion of Earth's magnetic field and is in many ways analogous to the effects of a magnetic storm. Looking forward, the USGS has proposed improving the U.S. magnetic monitoring systems and performing more detailed magnetotelluric surveys to better understand both EMP and magnetic storm hazards. Love also called for open access to power grid impact data to better understand how EMP and magnetic storms can affect engineered systems.

When asked if the power grid industry is doing something to address these hazards, Love replied yes, that the industry takes these magnetic storms seriously and has made progress that gives the industry operational flexibility during a magnetic storm. For example, when a coronal mass ejection occurs, which might produce a magnetic storm, grid operators will often add generating capacity to the system and be prepared to reroute electricity to keep the grid operating. He added that there are no plans to turn off the grid in response to a magnetic storm.

PLANNING FOR RARE EVENTS: SUPPORTING GOOD GOVERNANCE FOR RESILIENCE

Nestor Alfonzo Santamaria noted that unlike the previous speakers, who addressed specific types of rare events, his remit at OECD is to take an all-hazards perspective on planning for rare events. He explained that every country has its own way of planning for rare events, but there are common features of those approaches that include conducting a risk analysis to identify possible scenarios the country could face. These illustrative, rather than exhaustive, scenarios serve as a way for communicating the risks on which policy makers are concentrating. For example, some countries focus on natural hazards while others take an all-hazards approach.[4]

After conducting a risk analysis, countries engage in risk evaluation, which may also include involving specific ministries or agencies in the process of identifying the capacities needed and that should be prioritized to deal with the identified risks. Ultimately, each country then makes an investment decision based on the probability of an event occurring; the nature, intensity, and duration of the event; and the probability that the event would cause certain types of impacts. The risk evaluation process, said Santamaria, enables countries to understand and compare the significance of different risks on the basis of how likely they are and what their effects might be. Those two factors are captured in a likelihood/plausibility score and overall impact score, which together inform risk prioritization.

While some of this analysis includes complex mathematical models for naturally occurring events, many of the risks that countries worry about arise from threat vectors with malicious intent that do not have models. These two types of threats have different sets of uncertainties underpinning them, said Santamaria, which makes

---

[4] An all-hazards approach, as described in OECD's *Assessing Global Progress in the Governance of Critical Risks*, "allocates resources to risks that are most likely to have a national significance." The approach is not meant to mitigate all possible hazards, but is meant to address "known unknown" and "unknown unknown" problems. See OECD, 2018, *Assessing Global Progress in the Governance of Critical Risks*, OECD Reviews of Risk Management Policies, OECD Publishing, Paris.

the analysis challenging. To deal with this, the Swiss have grouped risks in clusters according to the monetary value of the damage that would result from those risks. This type of analysis starts with looking at the worst-case scenario, but based on recent events, such as the COVID-19 pandemic and the United Kingdom withdrawing from the European Union, it is clear that the worst-case scenario is highly variable and must change as new data become available. Brexit provided a different case example and required changing detailed models of personnel flows across borders that were included in models of COVID-19 transmission and spread, to inform a national security risk assessment.

The United Kingdom, the Netherlands, and Sweden have each gone through an exercise that plans for common consequences of various incidents, such as disruption to utilities, transportation, and health care, rather than having in place specific arrangements for responding to specific risks, remarked Santamaria. Ultimately, he explained, these exercises are about developing capabilities that are more generalizable, which represents a shift in the emphasis of developing specific capabilities to deal with specific hazards of various types.

These capabilities are more adaptive, and as an example, he noted that Spain is now looking at the mechanisms it needs to shift its national industrial and production capabilities to address needs as they arise and the social compact it needs to form with industry to respond to an unforeseen and rare catastrophic event. Instead of creating stockpiles to respond to specific events, Spain is investing in a process to understand how to mobilize its manufacturing capacity to address many types of challenges quickly when they arise. He also noted a similar OECD risk management review aimed to strengthen Paris's resilience to the risk of a catastrophic flood of the Seine River that would wipe out much of Paris.

Another challenge Santamaria referred to that is associated with risk planning is communicating how much of a challenge a risk could present. As an example, Denmark has established what it calls the "Pandora Cell," which tries to identify what could go wrong during a crisis and work out what the response might be if everything went wrong. This is intended to help crisis managers understand whether an incident could be getting worse, whether they could see a loss of control, and whether they could face resource shortages with a further spread of the crisis. This process involves gathering a team of experts to outline the problems that may worsen during an event and then identify three to five concrete issues that crisis managers need to look for during a serious event.

PLANNING AND RESPONDING TO SIGNIFICANT RARE EVENTS

Madhav Marathe's presentation focused on socially coupled networks, which are the networks that allow the flow of goods, services, people, finances, and information. These networks, explained Marathe, make the world more efficient in terms of the transfer of these types of commodities. Over the past 15 to 20 years, these networks have made the world "smaller" with the advent of communication systems, but the interconnected nature of these networks also creates situations that can lead to large-scale contagions and cascades. These cascades can spread across multiple sectors and nations, with significant social, economic, and human costs. The Chicago metropolitan area, for example, covers 400 square miles and includes 9 million people who depend on a transportation system with some 4 million edges and nodes that accommodates approximately 31 million trips; a social network for public health with approximately 20 million nodes in a temporal network with 1-second resolution; and a telecommunication system with 1 million IP addresses that handles some 125 million calls per day. Any model for planning and preparedness would have to account for all of these interconnections.

The first example Marathe discussed involved the urban transportation planning that would occur sometime after a 9/11-type event. The analysis was designed to understand the effect on traffic and the surrounding neighborhoods of closing streets around the White House. The project considered multiple solutions and considered the trade-offs between the effectiveness of an intervention, its costs, and the overall impact on travelers in the area.

The second example was a project his group conducted for DTRA as part of a national planning scenario in which a 10-kiloton weapon is detonated in downtown Washington, DC. Marathe's project focused on the social behavior and economic impact of this event between time zero and 3 days post-event. The models his team developed included power systems, the transportation system, the social context network, communications networks, building infrastructure, and the connections between these networks. Though these systems are huge, the resulting simulations suggested that small details matter and need to be presented in a meaningful manner.

In addition, observed Marathe, the modeling results showed that complex behavior adaptation is central to the risks in the first 3 days as people try to recover from what has happened. He noted that models such as this need to include various types of behavior changes that occur to escape, seek care, reconstitute households, estimate danger, or leave the area. Other findings from this project were that behaviors and the physical environment co-evolve and that information plays an important role in situational assessment and response coordination. Another thing the models showed was that even a partially restored communication system has a disproportionately positive effect on overall behavior and reducing anxiety. Partially restoring communication can be done today, he added, using what is known as a cell on wheels, which are networks that can be brought up quickly. This modeling effort also showed that although the power network would be completely destroyed in the area and not likely to be restored for 2 to 3 years, the cascading failure effect would be relatively minimal.

The third example Marathe discussed involved modeling pandemic response. In December 2020, this effort looked at how to optimally allocate a limited supply of vaccines. By February 2021, the work shifted to spatially modeling vaccine allocation in an efficient manner because the vaccine supply was plentiful by then.

In April 2021, this work shifted to understand the effect of new and emerging strains. Additionally, the Centers for Disease Control and Prevention (CDC) created a real-time scenario modeling hub focused on trying to understand what might happen under various scenarios extending a few months into the future. In June 2021, modeling was used to try to understand the risk of vaccine hesitancy. In July, this work started planning for evolving strains, in August the simulations looked at the effect of waning immunity, and in September the effort aimed to understand the impact of vaccinating 5- to 11-year-olds. In each case, the goal was to assess the epidemiologic outcomes for these scenarios given the current ground conditions.

What Marathe and his collaborators developed as part of this work is a novel platform that harnessed two supercomputers to do these simulations in close to real time. This involved building a large, agent-based modeling environment for the entire United States that is a digital twin of the nation[5] that includes a detailed representation of the underlying social contact network using data from various sources. This model is able to forecast how COVID-19 would spread in every state and county in great detail using current data on vaccine uptake according to demographics, hesitancy surveys, policies and interventions in place, and vaccine supplies.

One forecast from this model was that the effect of protection is relatively small if immunity wanes to the extent that it has following immunization or infection. This has turned out to be important with the appearance of the Delta and Omicron variants and shows the importance of booster shots. The model also forecasted that infections would peak between October and December 2021, which did start to happen until the Omicron variant appeared. Later forecasts that included Omicron suggested that infections would peak in early 2022.

In closing, Marathe emphasized that designing models for analyzing and anticipating future events should account for system resiliency, efficiency, and sustainability. System design, he explained, should be taught to include considerations of rare events. "While anticipating such events might be challenging or impossible, one can certainly try and prevent or delay or recover from it in a graceful manner," he asserted. Marathe also noted the challenge of modeling social systems that arise from co-evolution because of the fact that actions can change potential outcomes for many of these scenarios.

DISCUSSION

To begin the discussion, Santamaria asked Marathe if he has been able to track the performance of his model against the observed reality, particularly with regard to the sensitivity of the projected trajectory to certain specific interventions. Marathe replied that the forecasting model, which only makes projections out to 4 weeks, has done reasonably well in terms of confirmed cases, hospitalizations, and death when compared to the ground truth. Where his model and others struggle is when there is a sudden uptick in cases. With scenario modeling, there is no ground truth against which to compare performance, but such is not the purpose of that model. Rather, it serves to inform planning and efforts to make systems more resilient in the long run.

---

[5] "Digital Twin" does not imply that the model represents every single aspect of the nation's pandemic response, but rather that the model is updated regularly with real-world information, so that it remains current (in terms of vaccines, demographics, cases, deaths, etc.).

Marathe added that one issue that confounds planning is people forget when an event does not occur, which makes it difficult to sustain the investments needed to make systems resilient over the long term. That issue is compounded, said Santamaria, in democracies, where there is almost a disincentive to invest when that decision does not align with the political cycle. The decisions elected officials make depend at least in part on how their population is processing the situation, which can be contrary to what the model expects.

As a final comment, Santamaria said to beware of biases, particularly cognitive biases, because they can lead to the idea that there are certain measures that make sense to implement in a specific direction that may, in fact, not be the best path forward. "I think having explicit mechanisms to address cognitive biases is important in decision making, particularly for rare events," he said.

5

Fireside Chat—
Using Artificial Intelligence to Predict the Occurrence of Sepsis

To conclude Day 1 of the workshop, Madeleine Clare Elish, senior research scientist at Google, and Michele Wucker, co-founder and chief executive officer of Gray Rhino & Company and planning committee member, engaged in a conversation about work Elish did with the Sepsis Watch program prior to joining Google.[1] The conversation started with Elish explaining that sepsis, which develops when an individual's immune system becomes overactive when fighting an infection, is not rare. By one measure, sepsis is the leading cause of death in U.S. hospitals, and the World Health Organization recognizes sepsis as a profound health problem worldwide. A key feature of sepsis is that it is treatable when caught in time, but it is notoriously difficult to detect and treat quickly. In fact, there is no one test for sepsis or even one definition. "There are risks, rubrics, and protocols, but effectively treating sepsis remains a challenge for most hospitals," said Elish.

This, she stated, is where machine learning and AI can prove useful. Many groups have developed deep learning models trained on historical electronic health record data that will predict which patients are at high risk of developing sepsis, but most remain in the research phase. Sepsis Watch, however, has been integrated into the everyday operations of the Duke University emergency department to help improve patient care for those individuals who are at risk for developing sepsis.[2] Sepsis Watch, as Elish described, involves a deep learning model that appears to be working smoothly, and clinicians feel it has improved patient care for sepsis, though the associated clinical trial was just concluding at the time of this workshop.

Wucker cited a line from the Sepsis Watch research publication[3] that said, "AI interventions must always be thought of as sociotechnical systems in which social context, relationships, and power dynamics are central, not an afterthought," and she asked Elish to explain the concept of sociotechnical systems and how that concept played out in Sepsis Watch. Elish, a cultural anthropologist by training, replied that she sees the world as complex social systems where understanding culture, values, and beliefs are essential to understanding what people are doing and why they are doing it. This view is critical from a qualitative social sciences perspective, but it is often

---

[1] M.P. Sendak, W. Ratliff, D. Sarro, E. Alderton, J. Futoma, M. Gao, M. Nichols, M. Revoir, et al., 2020, "Real-World Integration of a Sepsis Deep Learning Technology into Routine Clinical Care: Implementation Study," *JMIR Medical Informatics* 8(7):e15182, https://doi.org/10.2196/15182.

[2] Additional information about Sepsis Watch is available at https://dihi.org/project/sepsiswatch and https://physicians.dukehealth.org/articles/dukes-augmented-intelligence-system-helps-prevent-sepsis-ed.

[3] M.C. Elish and A.W. Watkins, 2020, "Repairing Innovation: A Study of Integrating AI in Clinical Care," https://datasociety.net/wp-content/uploads/2020/09/Repairing-Innovation-DataSociety-20200930-1.pdf.

overlooked in technological interventions. The point she and other social scientists make in their research is that it is wrong to think about technology as neutral and separate from society. In fact, cautioned Elish, that perspective is dangerous because for a critical intervention to work, it needs to not just exist but actually work and achieve its goal. "It will fundamentally work better," she observed, "if we take into account how technical and social systems are complexly intertwined."

To Elish, the term sociotechnical is key because it shows how intricately and inextricably interrelated technical and social systems are. In the case of Sepsis Watch, this meant thinking not just about the deep learning model itself and the outputs of the model, but thinking about the larger system in which this model exists. That system, she added, includes the doctors and nurses who will use the model, as well as the power hierarchies, the existing organizational dynamics, and existing systemic issues or biases in health care systems generally.

Wucker shared that one insight in the paper describing Sepsis Watch that impressed her was that predictions do not exist in a vacuum, that if people respond to a prediction, the outcome will be different than when they do not respond to the prediction. She then asked Elish to talk more about that feedback loop. Elish added that when a patient arrives in the emergency department, their personal electronic health record is run through the Sepsis Watch model. If the model predicts that the individual is at high risk of developing sepsis, that patient's information is displayed on a patient card in the Sepsis Watch iPad app. The nurse who monitors the app and regularly checks for new patient cards calls the emergency department physician caring for that patient and conveys that elevated risk to the physician over the phone. If the emergency department physician agrees that the patient requires preemptive treatment for sepsis, the patient is tracked further and monitored on the iPad app to ensure that the recommended treatment is complete on time.

Elish noted that the treating physician does not directly see the Sepsis Watch model output, nor does the model produce a pop-up notice in the electronic health record. This workflow, she said, may seem Byzantine, but it was intentionally designed this way because the clinician leading this project had tried previously to develop sepsis care advisories that included such pop-ups, and the nurses routinely ignored them because of alert fatigue. As a result, the project was designed not just to use deep learning technology to produce better risk predictions, but to pair it with a human-facilitated intervention. To Elish, this is perhaps the most important takeaway from her work on the project—while this is a sophisticated AI intervention, it is linked in a thoughtful way that considers how it integrates into the workflow, and it includes a human who is responsible for ensuring that the model output affects patient care.

When Wucker encouraged her to talk more about the feedback loop between what the project team learned from the prediction system and how they then tweaked the system to make it work better, Elish responded that a unique feature of this project is that clinicians, not computer science experts, led the project. The two clinicians who led the project, in collaboration with a data science innovation center, had been working on improving sepsis care for years and had published papers about the alarm fatigue that doomed their previous interventions. The research team, she noted, was thoughtful about involving the expertise of stakeholders beyond physicians and about how the human and technical components would work together. Nevertheless, her research found there was a large amount of what she called disruption—breakages of communication and organizational norms that this new tool introduced into the setting. Sepsis Watch, she remarked, created this disruption and it needed the expertise of nurses to do what she called "repair work" to ensure that the disruptions and breakages Sepsis Watch created were effectively repaired to make the system work again.

Elish explained that the disruption Sepsis Watch produced was on purpose in that it disrupted the usual way of doing things in order to refocus how and when patients at risk of sepsis received care. While this disruption was productive, it required addressing the power differential between doctors and nurses and the fact that the nurses and doctors were in two separate locations, which meant the nurses did not know the physicians' rhythms and schedules. Initially, the nurses were calling at often inopportune times, but thanks to some impressive work, the nurses were able to develop effective communication strategies and understand better when the best times were to call the physicians. In this fashion, these issues were solved. This was not something the developers had thought of, she added.

Another factor the developers thought of was to design the output to simply categorize risk as high, medium, or low and not to provide an explicit diagnosis that might turn off some physicians. In this way, the physicians could take the output into account without feeling they were being told what to do. At the same time, the nurses took it upon themselves to read the patient's chart before talking to the physician so they could engage in a two-way conversation and be a partner rather than a threat to the physician's authority.

The Sepsis Watch paper notes that ground truth is hard to find regarding sepsis, and Wucker encouraged Elish to talk about why ground truth is important and what to do when it cannot be quantified. Elish replied that the ground truth issue stems at least in part from the lack of a uniform definition of sepsis. The CDC, for example, has one definition, and many hospitals have their own, different definition, which means there is no ground truth against which to train and judge a machine learning model. The way the Sepsis Watch team addressed this was thorough, careful, locally contextualized, multi-stakeholder decision-making using the standard that made the most sense to them, which was the Centers for Medicare & Medicaid Services' definition. The team modified the definition according to its own local knowledge and the local care context of the hospital's patients.

When Christopher Barrett commented that looking for a ground truth in an application such as this is pointless, Elish agreed to a point. Setting a ground truth was necessary in terms of training and evaluating the model, so the team had to pick something. She agreed, though, that this is about different ways to be situationally aware and the role of human decision-making relative to a particular context. This is a lesson that the AI and machine learning world still needs to learn. "It is not the output of this model that is helping doctors treat sepsis better. It is the whole system that is treating and helping improve patient care," she emphasized.

To end the conversation, Wucker encouraged Elish to talk about the role of power dynamics relative to acting on predictions. Elish responded that when she looked at the sepsis program and the idea of repair, it elevated the role of the human as being an important component of the system. The idea of a moral crumple zone, she said, arises when there is a human in the loop but not in an elevated position, which leads to underestimating the importance of the human and the situation going wrong. This is a situation that would be familiar to those who study complex systems with distributed control, something she has examined in the context of responsibility and liability associated with driverless cars. In that situation, the drivers end up in a moral crumple zone because they are charged with being responsible for the entire system, when control is actually distributed.

6

Fireside Chat— Rare Events and Insurance

Day 2 of the workshop began with a conversation between Michele Wucker and Markus Gesmann, co-founder of Insurance Capital Markets Research, which provides quantitative research on the global specialty reinsurance industry for insurance carriers, intermediaries, and investors. Wucker started the conversation by asking Gesmann to talk about the types of events on which reinsurance focuses. He first explained that specialty insurance is bespoke insurance for the risks for which a traditional insurance company does not have a standardized product, such as for a new solar park. Reinsurance is insurance for insurers to protect them against peak risks, such as earthquakes, wind storms, and other rare events. Both specialty insurance and reinsurance deal with rare events and risks for which there is little or no historical data.

Wucker commented that Gesmann's work involves the predictions insurers have to make, such as the probability that a certain event will occur and what its impact might be, or even what the effect will be on the particular companies that a client firm insures versus all insured in the same market. His work also has relevance to the capital markets because it helps manage the difference between what insurance companies see as the risk and the right pricing and what the markets see as the right risk and pricing. With that as context, she asked Gesmann how the reinsurance and specialty insurance industries address a situation for which there is little or no historically available information.

One approach, said Gesmann, is to find analogies. He pointed out that Lloyd's of London was the first company to insure a car, and the company treated the car like a ship that navigated on land. Another approach for insuring a portfolio of properties against windstorms is to use the historical record of storm tracks for the past century to inform the risk assessment. He then noted that when the first commercial airline flights were happening, someone came up with the idea of offering insurance for mid-air collisions. Although there was no historical data to go on, because such an accident had not occurred, a simple Bayesian model estimated the probability of a mid-air collision to be around 14 percent for any one year, which might seem high. However, there have in fact been 11 such incidents with more than 100 fatalities between 1955 and 2015, which shows that 14 percent was not a bad predictor after all: 11 events over 60 years equals 18 percent. The analogy he used was the lottery—the probability that any one person would win the lottery is remote, yet most every weekend, someone wins the lottery. In terms of setting a price for that insurance, the insurer will then need to figure out the probability that one of the planes it insures will collide with another plane based on its market share.

Gesmann explained the concept of risk sharing with the example of a terrorist attack on New York that destroys everything in a particular location. In that case, no one insurer would be able to cover the damage, so the industry practice is to syndicate the risk across many insurers spanning the globe. That led Wucker to prompt Gesmann to explain the logic behind terrorism insurance and how the industry thinks when there has been a lull between attacks or immediately after a big attack. The short answer, he replied, is that the perception of risk after a major event is often much higher than the actual risk in the insurer's mind, which creates an opportunity to charge more for such a policy. As a case in point, the World Trade Center attack was a disaster for the insurance industry, and many insurers retreated from the market. However, other companies felt prices would rise dramatically and they would make a great deal of money if they could tolerate the risk. The key here, said Gesmann, is to build resilience, which can be accomplished by accumulating cash, for example, or by diversifying the insurance portfolio and testing that diversification with portfolio modeling.

Wucker divulged that a few years ago, a friend of hers who worked on modeling virus outbreaks was talking with reinsurance companies about developing pandemic insurance. The companies looked into this quite exhaustively and not a single one decided to offer such a product, which proved to be a good thing for the insurers given what has happened since. Today, however, as Gesmann pointed out, the industry is looking into offering such a product because the perception of risk is high enough that insurers could charge a price that aligns with their risk models. Similarly, 30 years ago, a catastrophe modeler named Karen Clark was talking to insurers about the huge risk that a major hurricane would tear through Florida. Although they ignored her warning, Hurricane Andrew taught those insurers a lesson and completely transformed how the industry looks at natural catastrophes and risk and how it uses models to better understand that risk.

Wucker prompted Gesmann to explain how insurance companies factor near misses into their calculations, given that they only learn about incidents that occur, not how many times a policyholder was lucky. This is an issue for insurers, he replied. With hurricanes, the industry is constantly recalculating risks following each near miss using updated data on storm tracks. The auto insurance industry is benefiting in this regard by the increased use of telemetrics, the devices and apps that record a driver's behavior and can provide data about near misses. In a similar manner, he predicted that insurers would deploy Internet of Things devices on container ships to gather more information about how many storms a ship missed that could have caused severe damage. Being able to monitor behavior and the conditions in which it occurs will be transformative for the industry, Gesmann predicted.

He then told a story from 20 years ago when the Russian Mir space station was brought down into the Pacific Ocean. An American fast-food chain marked a 40-foot-by-40-foot target in the Pacific Ocean off Australia as part of an advertising campaign and announced that everyone in the United States would get a free coupon if Mir landed inside the target area. Because the cost of providing free food at the scale would be huge, the company sought to insure itself. Allegedly, the insurance firm the company engaged decided that the probability of this happening was so low that it did not matter how it priced the policy, but given that the company perceived the risk was high, the company decided to charge as much as it could. Similarly, David Aldous wondered how much Berkshire Hathaway charged to insure the billion-dollar payout if someone predicted all 64 results from college basketball's championship tournament. Gesmann replied he would look up the financial statement of the company offering that prize and determine how much they could afford. "That is how much I would charge," he said.

Mel Eulau, a senior program officer at the National Academies, asked if scenario-based mitigation strategies affect risk assessment for extreme events for which little or no data are available. Yes, replied Gesmann, for such an approach helps insurers limit their exposure to such events and it helps set prices for such insurance in relationship to the number of companies that are willing to accept a share of the total risk.

One challenge the insurance industry is facing today arises from global climate change. Insurers have used the huge historical weather database for its actuarial calculations, but as the past couple of years have demonstrated, the nature and frequency of extreme weather events is changing, casting doubt on the value of model outputs. A similar situation is developing in the auto insurance industry with the advent of self-driving cars. Gesmann said that what the industry is doing in these cases is to assess how credible the historical information still is, using Bayesian modeling techniques that can provide insights into how such changes affect a model's performance. He then took a moment to explain that Bayesian logic is just a formal approach of weighing the importance of different pieces of information and different assumptions to an outcome. For anyone interested in Bayesian concepts, Gesmann recommended two books—*Thinking, Fast and Slow*[1] by Daniel Kahneman, as a good introduction to

---

[1] D. Kahneman, 2011, *Thinking, Fast and Slow*, Farrar, Straus, and Giroux, New York.

Bayesian concepts, and the more advanced book *Statistical Rethinking*[2] by Richard McElreath for learning to apply Bayesian concepts and tools.

Robert Axtell from George Mason University commented that human behavior is often the most important component in determining an outcome and wondered if insurers conduct after-the-fact analyses to determine whether they missed something structural or whether some aspect of human behavior was missing from a given risk model. The way insurers include human behavior in their models, said Gesmann, is to go into the field and observe the roles humans play in an event. For example, before insuring a power plant, insurers will send engineers to the plant to see how the plant is run and if the control room is neat and tidy, which provides an indication of how the company operates.

Gesmann pointed out that over the past 20 years, the insurance industry had significantly changed the way it assesses risk and uses probabilistic programming, in part because of the dramatic advances in computational power that has occurred during that time. In addition, modeling has evolved from a simplistic approach to a risk-based approach, by which he meant that insurers had to build models to assess risks from a 1 in 200 scenario, and by incorporating Bayesian analysis using probabilistic programming languages such as Stan or PyMC.

Lastly, Gesmann suggested that making predictions is one thing, but getting people to act on them and spend money to insure against them is another. No one buys insurance because they want to, only because they have to do it. This is a particular problem with policy makers who have to balance spending money now to protect against a huge disaster that may or may not occur in the future.

---

[2] R. McElreath, 2020, *Statistical Rethinking: A Bayesian Course with Examples in R and STAN*, second edition, CRC Press, Boca Raton, FL.

7

Multisource Information Fusion, Situation Assessment, and Course of Action Selection

The first panel session on Day 2 featured three presentations on planning for and responding to an unanticipated rare event. The three speakers were Alice Hill, the David M. Rubenstein Senior Fellow for Energy and the Environment at the Council on Foreign Relations; Delores Knipp, research professor at the University of Colorado Boulder; and John Organek, director of operational architecture at the Electric Infrastructure Security Council. Vicki Bier, professor emerita at the University of Wisconsin–Madison and planning committee member, moderated a discussion period following the three presentations.

OVERCOMING FAILURES OF IMAGINATION

Alice Hill noted that although this workshop's focus is on rare events, such as pandemics and extreme weather events—the subjects of her recent research— these are no longer rare. It is notable that infectious disease experts have been predicting that the world was due for a pandemic, but even after close calls with Ebola, AIDS, SARS, and MERS, the world was not prepared for COVID-19. Similarly, climate scientists have been raising the alarm about climate change and the dire consequences it would have, but policy makers failed to take this warning seriously until the growing number of extreme weather events provided a taste of what the future holds without action.

Hill explained there are many cognitive reasons for why humanity keeps getting caught unprepared for these events that are no longer rare, with a major reason being that humans suffer from a failure of imagination. She remarked that behavioral economists have identified cognitive biases that impede human decision-making and lead to flawed decisions. "We need to figure out how to get over our innate optimism, which causes us to believe that climate change impacts will not particularly affect us, or our tendency to judge risk based on our own experience," said Hill. "The question is, how can we overcome these biases? Because they have meant that we are not ready even though the predictions are clear that these events will occur."

Two means of overcoming a failure of imagination are to use scenarios and to create more usable and publicly available data. Scenario analysis, Hill explained, uses defined stories to examine possible outcomes for the future. Given that future events may not resemble what has occurred in the past, scenarios can stimulate and discipline the imagination. Originally developed for military planning, scenario analysis is now a part of the planning process for a range of industries, including the fossil fuels industry. The Shell Corporation, taking this approach early on, created a climate change scenario in 1998 centered on a huge storm pounding the U.S. Atlantic coast so badly that it sparked young people into climate activism, the government into regulating fossil fuels, and litigation over who pays for the damages caused by climate change. "We have not seen that yet in a big scale, but we have certainly seen elements of what they imagined," said Hill.

Climate scientists' use of scenarios has underpinned their analysis of how different levels of emissions over time could affect projected climate impacts. Researchers have also used scenarios for pandemic planning. Hill explained that a 2006 special report in the *Harvard Business Review*[1] outlined the risks of a pandemic and the planning needed to respond to a pandemic, information that the business world, or policy makers for that matter, did not use to prepare for the current pandemic. This report recognized that a pandemic differs fundamentally from other more traditional business continuity risks in that it is not a discrete event, but rather an unfolding global event. The authors of this special report recommended scenario planning for gauging potential effects on product demand, corporate operations, and company financials.

The COVID-19 pandemic, said Hill, has triggered a new appreciation of scenario-informed planning among companies and governments as they have tried to imagine what the new normal will be like and how soon it might arrive. Similarly, worsening climate extremes have also sparked an interest in scenario-based planning. Investigators in New South Wales, Australia, for example, recommended greater use of scenarios following the devastating summer bush fires of 2019 and 2020. The investigators explained that scenario planning would allow the government to consider the potential for more significant and more extreme events, including worst-case scenarios, to quantify the risk, to understand the preparation required to respond, and to identify the policy or other innovations that could exacerbate or reduce the risk.[2]

For scenarios to be useful, they must rest on accurate, usable, and relevant data. Hill emphasized that in the climate world, acquiring those data will require an overhaul of how that information is produced. Current climate models, she explained, capture broad trends and do not make localized predictions. However, such predictions are exactly what municipal planners and those running facilities like power stations and wastewater treatment plants need to anticipate potential disasters, ranging from floods in Indonesia, to heat waves in Portugal, to a severe cold snap in Texas.[3]

Hill recalled a conversation she had with the part-time mayor of Perdido Beach, Alabama. This small town on the Gulf of Mexico is surrounded by water on three sides, and flooding caused by Hurricane Ivan eroded big chunks of the town's beach front. The mayor told Hill in 2013 that as a small-town mayor, she did not have a planning staff or any resources to know the size of the threats her town faces and the actions the town can take to protect its residents. "Almost a decade later, that information is still lacking about extremes at a particular location, and not surprising, adaptation to the extremes we are already seeing, much less those in our future, has lagged," said Hill. Indeed, in June 2021 the chair of the Adaptation Committee of the United Kingdom's Climate Change Committee described adaptation as "under-resourced, underfunded, and often ignored."[4] In short, the research response to date on adaptation has been too little, too removed, and too theoretical. "There needs to be a broader, open shift to apply science to local climate adaptation," she remarked.

The National Oceanic and Atmospheric Administration (NOAA) reported[5] that the United States experienced a record-breaking 20 climate disasters in 2021 that each caused at least $1 billion in damages. Globally, Hill explained, the tally for climate change–exacerbated disasters reached $210 billion in 2020. Investing in risk reduction before disaster strikes, however, can save enormous sums of money. In higher-income countries, every dollar spent on risk reduction saves approximately $6 in damages when done effectively. In lower-income countries, every dollar invested in more resilient infrastructure yields $4 in benefits. An alarming trend in the United States, however, is that migration is strongest into some of the nation's regions with the highest risk for climate-associated disasters, such as flooding and fires.

According to the Federal Emergency Management Agency, 65 percent of U.S. counties do not have disaster-resistant building codes, even though every dollar spent on constructing a building that meets stronger codes

---

[1] *Harvard Business Review*, 2006, "Preparing for a Pandemic," May, https://hbr.org/2006/05/preparing-for-a-pandemic.

[2] United Nations Office for Disaster Risk Reduction, 2020, *Final Report of the NSW Bushfire Inquiry*, July 31, https://www.unisdr.org/preventionweb/files/73305_finalreportofthenswbushfireinquiry.pdf.

[3] A. Hill, 2021, "COVID's Lesson for Climate Research: Go Local," *Nature* 595:9, https://doi.org/10.1038/d41586-021-01747-9.

[4] Ibid.

[5] NOAA, 2022, "U.S. Billion-Dollar Weather and Climate Disasters," National Centers for Environmental Information, https://www.ncei.noaa.gov/access/billions, doi: 10.25921/stkw-7w73.

saves $11 in damages following a bad event, observed Hill. Equally worrisome, she asserted, is that the United States does not have a model climate-resilient building code available for communities to adopt. She mentioned that without information about where and how damaging events are likely to unfold and how to build resiliently, choosing the right adaptations to invest in can resemble guesswork. However, the current 100 to 150 km^2 resolution of climate models is too large for planning purposes because an area that large can span several towns and different risks from extreme events.

It is not just discrete communities that need access to localized climate predictions, she remarked, given the growing vulnerability of supply chains to disruption that extreme weather events and the COVID-19 pandemic have demonstrated. This is not a newly recognized problem, either. In 2011, severe flooding in Thailand closed factories that produce 40 percent of the world's computer hard drives, which caused prices to double and squeezed computer manufacturers.[6] During the pandemic, the fact that China produces 90 percent of a key component needed to make penicillin caused worldwide shortages.

In Hill's view, investments in localized climate risk information should be a public good. She highlighted the fact that wealthier communities and businesses are already hiring their own expensive consultants to provide tailored climate risk information. For example, a client wanting information about its exposure to hazards such as floods, fires, and extreme heat could pay upward of $1 million for 1 year of services, while a large corporation could pay a much steeper price, she explained. Such for-profit systems leave poor communities without access to the information they need to prepare for climate risks. "Governments must work with academia, nongovernmental agencies, and the private sector to develop publicly available models and tools that give decision makers the basic information they need to keep themselves safe," said Hill.

High-income nations, including the United States, can catalyze the science of practical climate predictions, just as they did with vaccine development for COVID-19, explained Hill. The need for such tools is great, particularly among low-income countries, and it is time to apply science to develop local solutions to the global climate crisis, she concluded.

SEVERE SPACE WEATHER AS A SOURCE OF RARE EVENTS OF MAJOR SIGNIFICANCE

To remind the workshop of the material that Jeffrey J. Love discussed on the workshop's first day, Delores Knipp explained that Earth is subject to the whims of the Sun's atmosphere and the solar wind. Bursts of solar flares on the Sun's surface and solar wind (high energy, sub-nuclear particles that are ejected from the solar surface) can have a major effect on Earth's magnetic field and atmosphere. These originate in active regions, which humans have long observed as sunspots. The troublesome events that occur on Earth typically happen in a matter of minutes to 1 to 3 days after a solar flare. Active regions, Knipp described, are nests of complex magnetisms that fuel solar eruptions of energetic particles that can travel at relativistic speeds and penetrate spacecraft and Earth's atmosphere minutes later, followed by slower waves of magnetized ejected coronal mass. She noted that some of the worst disruptions occur when a series of multiple interacting bursts and ejections reach Earth.

Over the past 11 years, the NASA-European Space Agency jointly operated Solar Heliospheric Observatory has provided images of the active regions. Scientists are trying to use the information that this and other observatories produce to power AI and machine learning approaches to understand which of these active region events will develop into super events. One such event occurred in October 2003 when the flares from the active region ionized Earth's upper atmosphere for hours.

Another major event, in May 1967, produced powerful X-ray bursts and extreme radio emissions that triggered a blackout of the radar and radio communication systems that served as an early warning system against nuclear attack by the Soviet Union. While the Intelligence Community and combat command officers were trying to determine whether this blackout was an act of war, forecasters in the solar space weather forecasting center in the Cheyenne Mountain Complex—which had opened weeks before—were determining that a solar flare and associated radio burst of unprecedented strength was occurring and was the likely cause of the blackout. From speaking with Russian colleagues, Knipp learned that this incident led the government there to fund solar research for decades afterward.

---

[6] A. Hill, 2021, "COVID's Lesson for Climate Research: Go Local," *Nature* 595:9, https://doi.org/10.1038/d41586-021-01747-9.

A similar situation developed in August 1972 when a strong solar flare produced the fastest ejecta on record. The energetic solar particles blinded the satellites monitoring the Anti-ballistic Missile Treaty, produced strong disturbances in the U.S. electrical grid, and detonated some 4,000 mines that the United States had deployed around Vietnam during the war.

What worries Knipp is the realization over the past 5 years that these extreme energetic solar particle events can be much larger and more expansive, and the particles they produce can in all likelihood penetrate spacecraft. Of particular concern is that these events can occur from active regions as they move to the backside of the Sun. Her worry is that with the increasing number of satellites in low Earth orbit, one of these eruptive events will interfere with the monitoring systems that, among other tasks, track orbiting satellites to prevent collisions with other spacecraft or with orbiting debris. In her mind, such solar eruptions would be weapons of mass destruction for the low Earth orbit environment without ever directly harming a human. Following an event in 1989, for instance, it took weeks for satellite operators to reacquire some 2,000 orbiting satellites and pieces of space debris.

In closing, Knipp warned there are multiple threats from individual solar active regions and that humanity's increasing level of dependence on technology creates vulnerabilities that might extend to lower levels of space weather storms. At the same time, there is little shared knowledge about these vulnerabilities because much of this information is either classified or kept confidential by companies out of concern for revealing their vulnerability to competitors. In addition, the multi-year lulls between solar cycle maxima mean that operators and decision makers are under-experienced in terms of dealing with these events.

EXPERIENCES FROM BLACK SKY PLANNING

A black sky event, explained John Organek, is an electric grid outage that extends for more than 30 days and that affects a wide area spanning at least one of the three major grid interconnections. There can be both natural and intentional hazards that cause a black sky event, including a small disturbance if the grid reaches what is called the state of self-organized criticality. The blackout of August 2003 was an example of such an event.

The electric industry refers to a black start event as the need to restart a major sector of the grid after a complete shutdown. In Texas, following the February 2021 cold snap, the grid was 4 minutes, 37 seconds from being able to witness such an event, said Organek. Even though the industry has planned and frequently exercises for a black start event, there has never been an occasion to see what happens if it were to be executed. In the Texas event, as a worrying example, only 7 of the 13 emergency generators needed for a black start were available during the cold snap. He added that the communications sector shares much in common with the electric in terms of ubiquity and consequence, and it may be more conducive to study.

The two primary hazards that can cause a black sky event are the geomagnetic disturbances that Knipp and Love addressed and a high-altitude EMP from a nuclear detonation. Organek indicated that other hazards, such as a cyber-attack, a coordinated physical attack, or intentional electromagnetic interference, could further aggravate a black sky event, which fortunately did not happened during the Texas blackout. Such intentional, malicious attacks might also be more conducive to study in terms of being able to anticipate rare events, he said.

A black sky event, Organek warned, would have a major effect on DoD's mission to project force, both directly and through the cascading effects on other infrastructure, such as communications, transportation, and supply chains, as well as on the military enterprise itself. Fort Bragg, for example, is not only a critical installation for force projection, but it also sustains the equivalent of a city of 250,000 people and is a part of a larger community of people in the surrounding area. Beyond taking care of its own, DoD also plays a major role in helping civil authorities respond and recover, which is an undertaking that will certainly not only affect force projection capabilities, but also affect the internal view of what happens on installations. A black sky event would quickly blur the distinction between these two missions, warned Organek.

Regarding risk, his organization breaks it down into the threat, vulnerability, and consequences of an event to be able to assess risk more accurately. He noted that likelihood and probability play into each of these components. Emergence, Organek explained, is a special category of events that does not fit into the categories of natural and intentional threats. Emergence in the context of the electric grid is a sudden, no-notice collapse of a major portion of the electric grid. The August 2003 black sky event, which affected a large part of the Eastern United States and Canada, was an example of an emergent event. In that case, the system reached a state of self-organized criticality, and the collapse was triggered by some seemingly harmless event that caused and reinforced failures throughout the system.

Organized criticality, Organek explained, is relevant to what the Electric Infrastructure Security Council refers to as the meta-grid—the tightly connected infrastructures, supply chains, and communities that exist. "Our lives and our society have become nearly completely dependent on this meta-grid, which is not capable of being fully understood," said Organek. "Though progress is being made in understanding adaptive complex systems and self-organizing criticality, there is still a long way to go in terms of building the capacity to detect the signs of a complex system approaching criticality." As an aside, he mentioned that the work climate scientists are doing regarding the increasing occurrence of extreme weather events may be applicable to understanding organized criticality and the electric grid.

Valuing the consequences of an event is important because resources are limited, so decision makers need to prioritize actions. Organek noted that NOAA employs an approach to determine and optimize the value of individual programs and the overall program portfolio, which is based on the contribution a program makes to improve a warning about weather events and the overall portfolio. He suggested that this approach is something that DTRA should study.

Turning to information fusion and decision-making, Organek explained that the electric sector has long collected data from critical infrastructures, including the use of time-synchronized sensors that provide wide-area situational awareness, to manage its operations. As modeling of complex adaptive systems and computational capabilities has improved, researchers and grid operators have explored how to use those data to expand the scope and improve the quality of research. Toward that end, grid modelers are developing and refining innovative and more effective models that enhance the operational capabilities that can anticipate, assess, and react to disturbances. Organek expects more of this will be automated going forward. As the grid undergoes a major topological and physical transformation, these models need to transform accordingly. As they do, the insights they provide should prove valuable to other critical infrastructures, including the meta-grid.

Modeling, Organek emphasized, should be supplemented by ground truth and developed independently of the supervisory control and data acquisition system. It should also be informed by the engineers who design and build the physical systems that models are trying to reproduce. "You have to understand the physical processes that are taking place that have been built into the systems," he explained. Incorporating ground truth throughout the information cycle is vital not only to the security of the grid, but also to moving closer to a goal of being able to anticipate rare events taking place in a complex network of networks, he added.

Too often, Organek expressed, the focus is on monitoring a computer-generated image instead of the real thing. Attackers take advantage of this by exploiting the networks that gather fused data, including the sensors, to look for gaps in detection using adversarial machine learning techniques. They then use this knowledge to disrupt, damage, or destroy equipment that may require a long lead time to replace. Today, none of the cybersecurity protocols for major infrastructure components address the sensors, which they assume are functioning correctly.

Organek concluded his remarks by describing the following risks—gray rhinos, pink flamingos, black swans, and bias toward action. He cited that those risks lead to self-inflicted decision-making wounds.

The term *gray rhinos*, originally coined by Michele Wucker, refers to high-impact, highly probable, non-random, threats that are ignored despite leaving a trail of warnings and evidence. The 2021 Texas power grid outage was such an event.

Pink flamingos refer to known knowns that are often discussed and ignored by leaders who are trapped in organizational cultures and rigid bureaucratic decision-making structures.[7] The term was used to describe the failure of leadership to view military installations as combat platforms that support force projection instead of being simply industrial complexes where people work.

Black swans refer to unknown unknowns or an event or situation that is unpredictable as a major effect[8] and about which everyone agrees afterward was something for which there were actions that could have and should been taken to prevent it.

---

[7] Mad Scientist Initiative, 2018, "Black Swans and Pink Flamingos," May 10, https://madsciblog.tradoc.army.mil/51-black-swans-and-pink-flamingos/?replytocom=4029.

[8] Ibid.

Finally, there is bias toward action, which has the opposite effect of a black swan. *Bias toward action* occurs when operators become too familiar with and overly confident about dealing with an incident and fail to detect a rare event in the making when they take action prematurely. "We call it the ready, fire, aim syndrome," he stated.

Organek noted that he has been working with DTRA on EMP-related vulnerability, both for power stations and substations. As part of this work, his organization was able to show that if an 1859-sized event occurred, it would not, contrary to common belief, melt everything electronic. "We were able to determine how well the circuit breakers could withstand an EMP or how an EMP would diffuse itself within the structure of a power generator," he explained.

DISCUSSION

The discussion began with a question for Knipp about how to prepare for millennial events—that is, those expected to occur once in a thousand years. For a solar energetic particle event, she suggested there should be discussions with satellite designers, mission designers, and operators who have had experiences with spacecraft operating in the Van Allen radiation belts, a known harsh environment. In her opinion, those experiences can provide lessons in terms of what space operators think their systems can handle. While those discussions may be happening in the classified world, that knowledge needs to be shared with the broader audience that would be affected by an outage of the global navigation satellite system.

Hill, responding to the same question, reiterated her earlier comment that many of the events that concern those attending the workshop are no longer as rare as they use to be, which she believes is something that planners and strategists have not yet internalized. The Texas grid failure, for example, was not a surprise event, given that there had been previous freezes. Rather, she asserted, a choice had been made not to be prepared. "I think the psychological and political barriers to us addressing particular events worsened by climate change is holding us back," said Hill. "I think it is a critical area of study because those events will happen with rapidity." Similarly, she remarked that building codes, land use choices, and infrastructure investments are still being made based on the assumption that the climate of the past is the climate of the future. "We now have an unstable climate that will continue to become more unstable," she emphasized. "We are making choices today that are just plain poor."

As an example, she cited the $1 billion DoD invested in the U.S. Army Garrison on Kwajalein Atoll in the Marshall Islands. When building it in 2013, Knipp stated, that both DoD and its contractor said there was no need to worry about sea level rise. Shortly afterward, they realized there would be sea level rise that would inundate freshwater supplies with salt water.

Organek warned that one of the humbling factors of an extreme event is that past performance is not an indicator of the future. This has been true of the COVID-19 pandemic, where experts continued to think they could make predictions when this virus was something novel. When he served in the military, he learned to use the word *forecast* instead of *prediction* because it is impossible to accurately predict anything that has a component of probability. On the other hand, he said, it is possible to prepare to be in a position to better understand an event and take more effective and appropriate action. In his view, one such action would be to make better use of the growing Internet of Things and the sensing information it can generate. It should be possible, he said, to create a monitoring system that is more interactive and more capable of observing infrastructure in real time. The data that networked sensors generate can also power simulations of alternative futures that could inform actions to respond to future extreme events.

Wucker asked Hill to talk about whether responses are included in a feedback loop when considering the potential costs and consequences of an event. As an example, if Texas had been prepared for the freeze, how much would that have reduced the costs and consequences of the resulting power outage? One lesson from the pandemic, noted Hill, is that the economy's emphasis on efficiency left supply chains vulnerable, in part because that approach failed to build redundancy and resilience into the system so it could respond better when a situation unfolds differently than anticipated. Modelers, she noted, have not been able to identify the cascading compounding effects that follow from weather extremes or rare events. It was clear that the electric grid in California was not ready for the wildfires that have increasingly affected the state, and the grids shut down when there is a major fire, producing a cascading effect on the state's economy. The Northern California fires caused a major displacement of people, and 20,000 people have moved into Chico, which had a population of 100,000, resulting in crowded classrooms and roads. Current models, she explained, cannot quickly forecast these cascading events, which results in an underinvestment in preparation and in educating the public to understand that maybe they should not live in a fire-prone area where insurance is no longer available.

A workshop participant asked the panelists if they think that analysts, technologists, and decision makers should receive training in strategic foresight and how to act on past real-life experiences. Hill replied that under the U.S. Constitution, decisions about where and how people build rests with state, local, tribal, and territorial governments. That has created a moral hazard in terms of the choices about where to build and how to build because the local communities want that tax base. Today, local decision makers may assume the federal government will take care of any consequences that develop, and Hill suggested that the federal government could send strong signals that if communities want the maximum economic help after a disaster, they need to invest in risk reduction. In fact, the federal government decided in the 1960s that states are responsible for developments on coastal barrier islands if they want to allow that to happen. Vicki Bier added that individuals are compounding the moral hazard problem through their intolerance of being told where they cannot build.

Christopher Barrett asked the panelists to comment on how the nation can move from simulation and forecasting to action. Knipp replied that in the satellite protection world, the new generation of companies that are launching large constellations of small satellites are less concerned about losses. They assume that they will simply launch a replacement if they lose one satellite, even though destruction of one of their satellites could generate enough debris to trigger a cascade of collisions that would render specific orbital ranges unusable going forward.

Organek explained that the small water systems, one of which experienced a cyberattack in early 2021, do not have the capacity to conduct the analyses and take the necessary preparatory actions to deal with such an event. In his opinion, there is a need for pooling modeling resources, something the Environmental Protection Agency and the U.S. Department of Agriculture do, to help these smaller systems with preparedness. One approach for doing so would be to create a regional grant system that would enable groups of smaller systems to pool resources. He also mentioned that DoD has funding to help communities address some of these preparedness issues.

Bier noted that the social sciences have done research on how better to communicate risk to decision makers. Recently, she recalled, Francis Collins, the director of the National Institutes of Health (NIH), said he wished that NIH had invested more in studying human behavior,[9] and a noted sociologist pointed out that sociologists have been saying that for a long time.

---

[9] *PBS News Hour*, 2021, "Dr. Collins Reflects on Career at NIH, COVID Response Effort, Work on Genome Sequencing," December 20, https://www.pbs.org/newshour/show/dr-collins-reflects-on-career-at-nih-covid-response-effort-work-on-genome-sequencing.

8

Active Prevention and Deterrence

The workshop's final session sought to tie together the lessons from the previous systems by addressing approaches to actively prevent and deter unanticipated rare events of major significance. The three speakers in this session were Terik Daly, senior scientist at the Johns Hopkins University Applied Physics Laboratory; Seth Baum, co-founder and executive director of the Global Catastrophic Risk Institute; and Robert Axtell, professor of computational social science at George Mason University. Justin Kasper, deputy chief technology officer for BWX Technologies and a member of the planning committee, moderated the final discussion after the three presentations.

ASTEROID IMPACTS—THINKING ABOUT AN UNCERTAIN THREAT

Large asteroid impacts are rare, but they are a legitimate concern, announced Terik Daly, who illustrated his point with a map of fireballs reported by U.S. government sensors. While most of the asteroids that enter Earth's atmosphere explode with little consequence other than a bright flash, the 20-m diameter asteroid that exploded over Chelyabinsk, Russia, in 2013 broke glass, caused structural damage across the metropolitan area, and sent a couple thousand people to the hospital. An event of that size, observed Daly, probably occurs every few decades to centuries.

In the early 1900s, an asteroid of diameter 60 to 190 m exploded in the atmosphere with the equivalent energy of 5 megatons of dynamite. This event occurred over an area that was unpopulated at the time, but it would have been a significant event if it had occurred over a population area. An event of this size likely occurs every few centuries to millennia, Daly noted. Going back 65 million years, the Chicxulub asteroid, which was 10 to 15 km in diameter, devastated Earth and led to the demise of the dinosaurs. This size event may occur every few hundred million years.

In thinking about this threat and how to evaluate it, Daly said it is important to remember that the likelihood and consequences of an asteroid impact varies with asteroid size. Small asteroids, about 4 m in diameter, enter Earth's atmosphere around once a year and are not a concern. Estimates place the number of these small asteroids at around 500 million, with fewer than 0.1 percent discovered. At the other end of the size spectrum lie the four huge asteroids that are 10,000 m or larger in diameter and the 900 or so asteroids between 1,000 and 10,000 m in diameter. These asteroids would cause global devastation, but they are also not a concern because astronomers know where more than 90 percent of these are and know they are not headed to Earth.

The asteroids of primary concern are those that fall between 50 and 1,000 m in diameter because these are large enough to cause regional devastation, they happen frequently enough—every 2,500 to 20,000 years or so—and most of the estimated hundreds of thousands of them remain undiscovered. "We think there are 200,000 asteroids 50 m or so that could come near Earth, and we have found 8 percent of them," remarked Daly. As an example of what a 50-m asteroid would do, he noted that an asteroid that size collided with Earth in what is now Arizona and left a crater that was 1.2 km wide and 180 m deep. Modeling shows that the devastation from this asteroid impact would have extended as far as 40 km. The fireball produced by the impact would have incinerated everything within about 10 km, killed or wounded all the large animals out to 24 km, and produced hurricane-force winds out to 40 km.[1] If a similar event were to occur over Washington, DC, the entire city would be incinerated in the fireball, with significant casualties throughout the surrounding areas in Maryland and Virginia.

Daly explained that the asteroid threat has been known for some time, and the understanding of that threat has not changed much over the past couple of decades. However, in 2016 NASA established a Planetary Defense Coordination Office, and in 2018 the federal government released a national strategy.[2] The strategy has five goals:

1. Enhance near-Earth object (NEO) detection, tracking, and characterization capabilities.
2. Improve NEO modeling, predictions, and information integrations.
3. Develop technologies for NEO deflection and disruption missions.
4. Increase international cooperation on NEO preparation.
5. Strengthen and routinely exercise NEO impact emergency procedures and action protocols.

In 2021, the White House released a report on NEO impact threat emergency protocols.[3]

Addressing the threat of an asteroid collision boils down to three things, explained Daly: find the asteroids, develop ways to prevent an impact or reduce its effects if it cannot be prevented entirely, and decide how to act in the face of massive uncertainties. For the first step, ground-based telescopes around the world are scanning the skies looking for NEOs. Over the past 8 years or so, the number of discoveries per year have plateaued even though new telescopes have come online during that time. "We have reached the limits of what we can do from the ground," he added. "At this rate, it will take decades before we can find all those asteroids large enough to cause regional devastation."

To address this, NASA is developing a space telescope to accelerate the hunt for these asteroids. The NEO Surveyor has a launch readiness date of 2026 and is designed to find asteroids 140 m in diameter and larger that come near Earth. Daly explained that 140 m is the threshold above which there would be massive consequences should one strike a major metropolitan area. Currently, astronomers have found 39 percent of these objects, and the mission's goal is to find 66 percent of them within 5 years of launch, with an aspiration of finding 90 percent of these objects within 10 to 12 years of launch.

He then explained how these numbers are derived and how astronomers know when they have hit these goals. "What we do is look at what we have found compared to what we think is out there," he said. Estimates of the population of NEOs come from extrapolating from observations of asteroids exploding in the atmosphere and understanding the collisional evolution of the solar system.

In terms of developing ways to prevent an impact, there are a few techniques that might work, with the options depending on the size of the asteroid and how much warning time exists.[4] For the largest asteroids with years

---

[1] D.A. Kring, 2007, *Guidebook to the Geology of Barringer Meteorite Crater, Arizona (a.k.a. Meteor Crater)*, Lunar and Planetary Institute, Houston, TX, http://www.lpi.usra.edu/publications/books/barringer_crater_guidebook.

[2] National Science and Technology Council, 2016, *National Near-Earth Object Preparedness Strategy*, Interagency Working Group for Detecting and Mitigating the Impact of Earth-Bound Near-Earth Objects, December, https://www.nasa.gov/sites/default/files/atoms/files/national_near-earth_object_preparedness_strategy_tagged.pdf.

[3] National Science and Technology Council, 2021, *Report on Near-Earth Object Impact Threat Emergency Protocols*, The Interagency Working Group on Near-Earth Object Impact Threat Emergency Protocols, January, https://trumpwhitehouse.archives.gov/wp-content/uploads/2021/01/NEO-Impact-Threat-Protocols-Jan2021.pdf.

[4] National Research Council, 2010, *Defending Planet Earth: Near-Earth-Object Surveys and Hazard Mitigation Strategies*, The National Academies Press, Washington, DC.

of warning, a nuclear detonation either on or next to an asteroid could disrupt it enough to change its orbit. This approach should also work for smaller objects without much warning time. The kinetic impact option—taking a spacecraft and slamming it into the asteroid—can be effective over a wide range of warning times. With many decades of warning, a gravity tractor would work. This involves parking a spacecraft next to an asteroid and letting the gravity of the spacecraft over decades slowly change the asteroid's orbit. If the NEO is small enough or there is not enough warning time for the above options, the option is civil defense involving preparing evacuation and effective response and recovery strategies.

On November 23, 2021, NASA launched the Double Asteroid Redirection Test (DART) mission to determine whether the kinetic impact approach can work. The spacecraft, whose core is about the size of a vending machine, will self-direct itself to crash into the 160-m Dimorphos asteroid that is orbiting around the larger Didymos asteroid. NASA is conducting this test at this double asteroid as a safety precaution, explained Daly, because the end result, if successful, will be to change the orbit of the smaller asteroid around the larger asteroid, not of the larger asteroid around the Sun. A small, shoebox-sized CubeSat called the Light Italian CubeSat for Imaging of Asteroids will fly over the asteroid and witness the impact. The goal is to change the orbital period of Dimorphos, as observed using ground-based telescopes, by about 1 percent.

In terms of deciding how to act in the face of massive uncertainties, Daly discussed a theoretical exercise conducted in 2019 that started with an asteroid discovered in March that had a 0.002 percent chance of impacting Earth in April 2027. Over the next month, additional observations increased the probability of a strike to 1 percent. At this early stage, the most likely thing to happen is that the asteroid does not hit the Earth, but decision makers will struggle to decide what to do to prepare for the unlikely event that it does hit Earth with major consequences. By July 2019, additional observations put the likelihood of impact at 10 percent, but it was not until 17 months later, in December 2021, that the impact probability had risen to 100 percent. At that point, decision makers had to decide how to reroute critical infrastructure and who to evacuate. In this exercise, the decision was made to try to deflect the asteroid, but that ended up being only partially successful. Impact occurred in 2027.

The national plan, noted Daly, provides guidelines on how to make decisions in the face of these large uncertainties based on four factors: how large, how likely, how soon, and how feasible is it to do anything to change the asteroid's trajectory. Looking at the interplay of these four factors leads to different actions, such as simply cataloging the asteroid, warning the public of an impending impact, preparing emergency responses, launching a mission to study the asteroid and more accurately determine its mass and orbit, or launching a prevention mission.

In closing, Daly added that there are no known asteroids that pose a threat to Earth for at least 100 years. However, he added, "we know we do not know where most of the asteroids are that could cause regional devastation." As a result, policy makers need to make decisions about how to deal with the threats that acknowledge both of those truths. "We have to allocate resources in a way that recognizes that right now there is no immediate threat, but also that we do not know where the asteroids are," finished Daly. "Once we do, which hopefully will be in the next decade, we will definitely know whether or not we need to be concerned about asteroids, but until that time, we have to make decisions and allocate resources in a way that addresses both what we know and what we do not know."

THE CHALLENGES OF ADDRESSING RARE EVENTS AND HOW TO OVERCOME THEM

From a big picture perspective, life on Earth will no longer be able to exist in about a billion years as a result of the Sun's natural stellar evolution that will have it become larger and warmer, announced Seth Baum. The interesting question, then, is what happens between now and then. There might be good developments such as advanced transformative technology breakthroughs and colonization of space, and there might be extreme catastrophes, such as the collapse of agriculture or industry, that could harm human civilization or lead to human extinction.[5] Discussions about global catastrophic risk, remarked Baum, focus on those catastrophes that cause harm on that scale. "There is a strong case for attention to this class of risk based on the important role that it can play in the big picture future of human civilization," he observed.

---

[5] S.D. Baum, S. Armstrong, T. Ekenstedt, O. Häggström, R. Hanson, K. Kuhlemann, M.M. Maas, et al., 2019, "Long-Term Trajectories of Human Civilization," *Foresight* 21(1):53–83, https://doi.org/10.1108/FS-04-2018-0037.

Addressing global catastrophic risk, Baum detailed, first requires understanding the possible decision options and how well they would work at avoiding that risk and then putting those options into action. The second step requires either motivating people or institutions to care about these extreme, catastrophic events or achieving action without motivating people to care about human civilization in the distant future.

Identifying and evaluating decision options is a significant challenge because of how rare and extreme catastrophic events are given that modern, global human civilization has never been destroyed. Baum remarked that this is obviously a good thing, but it does create a data problem, and it eliminates the option of making a data-driven, quantitative risk analysis. Fortunately, he noted, this type of analysis is not always needed. For instance, there are scenarios in which a nuclear terrorist attack could result in a nuclear war even if that was not the intention for many of the parties. This might happen if the victimized country misinterprets the attack as one from a rival country or one sponsored by a rival country and launches its own nuclear weapons in what it believes is retaliation, but is in fact, the start of a nuclear war.[6]

This scenario, Baum explained, is perhaps the only way that an extreme global catastrophe would result from nuclear terrorism. As a result, the policy conclusion should be that if there is going to be a nuclear terrorist attack in the future, there should be guardrails in place to ensure it is not an attack from another country so as to not accidentally initiate a nuclear war for the wrong reasons. "This is a policy conclusion that is not sensitive to doing a quantitative risk analysis," said Baum. "It is just a fairly obvious conclusion from this particular circumstance."

An example of when a quantitative analysis is needed involves nuclear power. Nuclear power is helpful for reducing greenhouse gas emissions, but at the same time, there are concerns that it can lead to nuclear weapon proliferation, which was the concern regarding Iran's nuclear program. These two factors require analyzing whether the benefits of reducing greenhouse gas emissions offset the harms related to nuclear weapon proliferation.[7] Quantitative analysis is important in this case to assess which of these two different effects is the stronger one and point to a clear answer as to whether nuclear power is a good thing or bad thing in any particular circumstance, Baum observed.

Baum presented a case he has previously studied—the use of nuclear explosives for asteroid deflection. In this case, the analytical question is whether the benefits of reducing the risk of an asteroid colliding with Earth offsets any harms that may arise from international security concerns. The conclusion he reached in his work is that while there is not a precise answer, there is much to learn from going through the analysis in terms of the various aspects of the risks and possible policy decisions that can better inform the decision-making process. He pointed out that in doing this research, he was not making any decisions about using nuclear explosives for asteroid deflection.[8]

Baum underlined that his group has been active in characterizing the risk of nuclear war and has developed a model for the probability of it.[9] The model outlines two paths to nuclear war, one in which there is an intentional first strike, the other involving unintentional or inadvertent nuclear war scenarios, such as the terrorist scenario he previously discussed. To inform the model, Baum and his collaborators compiled data from past nuclear war incidents, including World War II, and a long list of near-miss incidents that went part of the way to nuclear war, such as the Cuban Missile Crisis. These near-miss incidents, he remarked, go part of the way to determining the probability of nuclear war developing from relatively normal conditions to an initial event such as the Cuban Missile Crisis, but they do not fill in the remaining steps from that initial event to the decision to launch nuclear weapons. Nonetheless, this type of model can provide some understanding of the factors that might lead to nuclear war. He noted that he has also created a model for the effects of nuclear war on human population but would not discuss it in the interests of time.[10]

---

[6] S.D. Baum, 2018, "Uncertain Human Consequences in Asteroid Risk Analysis and the Global Catastrophe Threshold," *Natural Hazards* 94:759–775, https://doi.org/10.1007/s11069-018-3419-4.

[7] R.H. Socolow and A. Glaser, 2009, "Balancing Risks: Nuclear Energy and Climate Change," *Daedalus* 138(4):31–44, https://www.amacad.org/publication/nuclear-energy-climate-change.

[8] S.D. Baum, 2019, "Risk-Risk Tradeoff of Nuclear Explosives for Asteroid Deflection," *Risk Analysis* 39(11):2427–2442, https://doi.org/10.1111/risa.13339.

[9] S.D. Baum, R. Neufville, and A. Barrett, 2018, "A Model for the Probability of Nuclear War," Global Catastrophic Risk Institute Working Paper 18-1, https://gcrinstitute.org/papers/042_nuclear-probability.pdf.

[10] S.D. Baum and A.M. Barrett, 2018, "A Model for the Impacts of Nuclear War," Global Catastrophic Risk Institute Working Paper 18-2, https://gcrinstitute.org/papers/043_nuclear-impacts.pdf.

Returning to the question of how to achieve action to address these types of risks, Baum first discussed the nuclear terrorism scenario. He noted he could make a case for de-emphasizing the risk of nuclear terrorism except when it could lead to nuclear war, and some might find this argument persuasive and turn their focus to nuclear war, while others would not and would remain focused on the risk of nuclear terrorism. When two groups do not have the same motivation to focus on the risk of nuclear war, one approach is to draw attention to the scenario of nuclear terrorism leading to nuclear war. This approach can highlight ways to reduce the risk of an extreme global catastrophe without changing either group's primary focus.

As a second example, he discussed the trade-offs between the greenhouse gas benefits of Iran's nuclear power program and the proliferation risk. Here, the trade-off is less clear, and there is no obvious good answer to this question. At the same time, if the goal is to reduce greenhouse gas emissions, there is a long list of other possible actions, including expanding nuclear power in the United States where there is no nuclear weapons proliferation risk since the nation already has nuclear weapons and nuclear power. The same would apply to Russia and China. In fact, there is a project to have the United States and China cooperate to expand nuclear power to offset the use of coal, which he said would be a good development in terms of addressing climate change.

At the same time, there may be individuals who are not concerned about climate change, nuclear weapons, and global catastrophe. Another way of grounding this policy decision would be to emphasize the local benefits of exchanging nuclear power for coal-burning power plants in terms of reducing air pollution. "This is another way that certain actions can be achieved without necessarily having the same sort of motivation to address the rare events."

DEALING WITH EXTREMES IN ECONOMICS AND FINANCE

Economics and finance, asserted Robert Axtell, have a long and significant history of significant, rare events. Unlike the possibility of satellite collisions or the existence of rare biological species, in human social systems the probability of an extreme event, like a market crash, may depend on people's beliefs about such an event. This makes forecasting and anticipation inherently different for social systems, compared to natural systems, and notions such as *prevention* and *deterrence* may even be problematical for economic systems, in which fluctuations are a common feature of normal operations. While such events cannot be prevented, they can be managed.

The financial world has always lived with large, rare events. The Great Depression was one, as was the period of high inflation and unemployment during the 1970s, the financial crisis of 2007 to 2008, and the economic downturn triggered by the COVID-19 pandemic. These large events are part of distributions of events by size that are not Gaussian in character and are not fully understood, explained Axtell. The lesson here, he revealed, is that extremes are regular features of economic and financial processes.

The economic world, which is where his work focuses, is often dominated by extremes. For example, in the United States, there is one business firm with a million employees and nearly a million firms with one employee. Approximately 60 percent of U.S. private-sector workers are employed by the largest 1 percent of companies, and 80 percent of all people working for businesses are at one of the largest 10 percent of firms. Furthermore, these firms are linked through buyer-supplier networks. What this means is that fluctuations that happen in a few large firms, whether on short or long time scales, can have ripple effects throughout the entire economy. Axtell referred to this as the so-called granular hypothesis, due to Xavier Gabaix, which suggests that fluctuations among firms at the extreme end of the firm size distribution can be amplified macro-economically.[11] This holds true, he said, in the broader social world as well, where there are highly skewed distributions of city size, income, and wealth, as well as in the internet and social media worlds, where heavy-tailed distributions are associated with web connectivity, the numbers of friends and followers, and many other network properties.

To illustrate how rare economic and financial events manifest themselves in important ways, Axtell discussed several specific events. As a first obvious case, the stock market crash of 1929 led to the Great Depression and a decade-long loss of economic output. Another case was the tech bubble of 2000 to 2002, which led to a recession and to the Federal Reserve maintaining low interest rates for a long period. The subsequent sub-prime mortgage bubble resulted in nearly $10 trillion of losses to U.S. households.

---

[11] X. Gabaix, 2011, "The Granular Origins of Aggregate Fluctuations," *Econometrica* 79(3):733–772, https://www.jstor.org/stable/41237769.

While these are examples of how financial events can manifest themselves in the real economy and society generally, the opposite can also be true. For example, a decline in the output of silver mines in the early 1890s was partially responsible for the financial panic of 1893, which triggered bank failures in Chicago and New York. Other examples include the oil embargoes of the 1970s that led to dramatic swings in the value of commodities.

All of this is background, noted Axtell, to addressing the question of how to manage in a world with such extremes. He noted that for the first 100 or so years of U.S. history, booms and busts occurred every 4 to 5 years. Since the Great Depression and the empowerment of the Federal Reserve System, the period between recessions grew to 6 to 10 years, aided by various policy tools, like bank account guarantees, which effectively eliminated bank runs by depositors.

Axtell explained that many of these policies act in ex ante fashion—that is, they are actions taken ahead of time based on forecasts of how the economy is likely to respond to specific events and policies. When it comes to modeling social systems and forecasting policy actions, models have to represent how people will respond to policies. To cite one example, models of investors have to include policy maker behavior, and vice-versa, all conditional on how the world is likely to unfold. This back-and-forth between agents in the economy and policies makes rare economic and social events different from naturally occurring rare events.

It is also possible to manage financial extremes in real time, ex post, as when a big event occurs and action must be taken, remarked Axtell. Note that during the Black Monday event of October 19, 1987, stock market circuit breakers kicked in to stop trading temporarily until market panic receded and prices were re-established. Regulators can also intervene when particular firms get in trouble, as happened during the Asian and Russian financial crises of the late 1990s, when Long-Term Capital Management needed to be recapitalized, and then again during the financial crisis of 2008 when regulators bailed out certain banks that were "too big to fail" and arranged sales of troubled institutions. Subsequently, in the early days of high-frequency stock trading there were so-called flash crash events when prices of specific issues fell dramatically for brief periods and then quickly recovered. Such events were managed by the Securities and Exchange Commission (SEC) and Commodities Futures Trading Commission (CFTC) and through trading curbs. In the 1980s, regulators prosecuted bad actors involved in the savings and loan (S&L) crisis, after the fact, and today, the SEC can invalidate transactions it believes occurred for "insider trading," among other things. Axtell observed that there are a variety of ways to manage these rare events after they occur.

Another way to deal with financial extremes is to design systems to function in new ways in order to avoid extreme outcomes. In one case, the SEC ordered NASDAQ to get rid of trading in eighths and sixteenths of a dollar, hoping to eliminate so-called spread clustering by market-makers, among other objectives. At the time a "digital twin" of the NASDAQ was created in an attempt to forecast what would happen when the NASDAQ market decimalized.

Axtell pointed out that financial markets are in a constant state of evolution, creating growing complexity and meaning such markets can be hard to manage properly. For example, there are now "upstairs" markets in which big firms conduct large block trades without going through the trading floors of normal stock exchanges, meaning such transactions are often invisible to other market participants. Shadow banking is another relatively recent innovation in which financial activities occur among non-bank financial institutions and outside of the purview of normal regulatory authorities. Cryptocurrencies and blockchain capabilities are yet other innovations with the potential to disrupt normal market operations. All these innovations suggest that extreme economic and financial events are almost certainly as likely to manifest themselves in the future as they have in the past, albeit possibly for different reasons.

Beyond financial examples, Axtell observed that societies create institutions to manage rare economic events. Unemployment insurance payments help individual households and keep aggregate demand up during downturns. Bankruptcy laws exist to deal with the extreme event of a company going out of business. When the COVID-19 pandemic hit and restaurant and entertainment employees lost their jobs, a variety of legislation was put in place to help the people most affected.

To conclude his presentation, Axtell discussed whether reaction, mitigation, and adaptation might replace anticipation, prevention, and deterrence in the context of human systems. Modifying systems to prevent a bad outcome, can end up creating a system where there is a high chance that an even bigger failure can occur. As an example, the prevention of small fires in a forest may create the conditions for much larger fires to occur down the road. "By eliminating a certain class of events, do we effectively guarantee the occurrence of more extreme events?" asked Axtell.

In economics and finance, the idea behind trying to manage a complex system sometimes means doing it from the bottom up. In this approach, social science-savvy, behavioral solutions replace "technical" solutions, as the latter tend to be brittle and narrow, often leading to unintended consequences. For policy, Axtell explained, such unintended effects should be studied as first-order phenomena that may jeopardize the welfare gains produced by the policies in question. In that regard, Axtell emphasized that it is important to consider social welfare functions existing on individual, organizational, and societal levels.

Regarding deterrence, Axtell observed that deterrence and its relationship to mutually assured destruction was center stage during the Cold War, but in asymmetric situations deterrence is a more nuanced concept that takes on a different character. Consider new technologies that, when introduced, are not hardened and thus are vulnerable to hacking by adversaries. As examples, he cited how Gutenberg's invention of the printing press led to the Reformation, anonymous broadsheets attacking public figures, political strife, and yellow journalism; how advances in chemistry in the 19th century were "hacked" to produce chemical warfare during World War I; and how the invention of the internet led to social media platforms that are now organizing venues for extremists. These outcomes, resulting from new technologies having unintended consequences, are hard to see ahead of time or deter once they are used for hostile purposes.

Axtell then mentioned an idea circulating in economics and finance, concerning whether it is possible to create models analogous to weather forecasting that would take 70-plus years of economic experience and use supercomputers to provide a near-term forecast of possible outcomes. For weather, 2 weeks of look-ahead is now possible. High-fidelity modeling of the financial system might make it possible to computationally generate every type of economic or finance crisis possible, something that would be useful to agencies such as the Financial Stability Oversight Council or other institutions tasked with promoting robust market operations.

He then posed the idea of adopting a perspective that treats ideologies as platforms for action in the same way that YouTube or Facebook are platforms. The New York Stock Exchange and NASDAQ, for example, are platforms on which different customers operate. In that view, Axtell wondered if it is useful to think of democracy and authoritarianism as two platforms, or to consider capitalism, market socialism, and communism as platforms. The idea then would be to conceptualize the transition from one platform to another as a rare event.

In closing, Axtell concluded that in social, economic, and financial systems, rare events are simply events that occur in the tails of heavy-tailed distributions. Such events are managed in both ex post and ex ante fashion, by policy professionals, with more or less success. He explained that reaction, mitigation, adaptation, and redesign are more common in these areas than anticipation, prevention, and deterrence, which suggests that, say, eliminating all forest fires would be less effective than a strategy of keeping small fires from becoming catastrophic events. Given that the world is an ecology of adversarial agents who are perpetually evolving, new strategies are hard to anticipate, making deterrence hard in practice. However, computational modeling with rich data may provide better insights into rare events and how to manage them than the more heuristic methods used historically.

DISCUSSION

The discussion started with Daly answering questions about whether an adversary could turn an asteroid into a weapon and whether deflecting an asteroid might cause it to hit one country over another. Theoretically, said Daly, it would be possible to change an asteroid's path in such a specific way that it would strike a specific country, but from a practical context he said it was not obvious how that would work. Regarding the second scenario, that could be a possibility and a United Nations conference in 2020 actually wrestled with this issue.

Daly noted that the reason NASA runs the United States planetary defense system is so that these issues would be handled in the public eye rather than in secret through DoD. In fact, he stated, there are concerns about what China is doing in terms of planetary defense. The way to stay on top of what other countries are doing is to look at the technology developments that are occurring, he added.

Justin Kasper noted that plasma physics sees long-tailed distributions similar to those that Axtell discussed and added that they arise through long-distance interactions. He asked Axtell if economic models incorporate long-distance interactions among people and if that complicates trying to predict what groups of people will do. Axtell replied that data on who is interacting with whom over what distance do not exist, but such phenomena do exist. The collapse of Long-Term Capital Management was such an event where several coupled events occurred that triggered the company's default. He added that turbulence in financial markets is one of the few areas where the natural sciences and social sciences have a direct relationship. Kasper noted that this could be an example where the behavior of plasmas could be the analogous situation to inform finance and economic models since their statistics are similar.

When asked if there is a role for dystopian science fiction in developing scenarios of rare, high-impact events, Baum emphasized that the answer is definitely yes. One role science fiction can play is to help understand how some unprecedented catastrophes could play out. Another role is through public communication by making a particular risk more psychologically available in people's minds. For example, *Deep Impact*, the asteroid collision blockbuster film, played a constructive role in raising the public profile of the asteroid risk and may have led to some constructive policymaking. The danger is that science fiction might give people the wrong impression about the risk.

Baum then replied to a question about how much of the probability of the risk of nuclear war is driven by geopolitical events transpiring and how much is driven by bad procedures with logical flaws that result in a human doing something wrong. He remarked that this is a subject of contention within the nuclear war community and that there is currently no clear answer to that question. This is an important policy question, though, that could benefit from more research.

Kasper then asked the panelists to comment on the role that high-fidelity digital twins might play in better understanding the particular risks they study. Daly replied that it is important not to trust the digital twin too much. He suggested that the asteroid community assumes in its simulations that asteroids are made of quartz and that spacecraft are made of aluminum, neither of which is completely true. He noted, too, that people outside of the community might look at the visualizations a digital twin produces and believe they must be right, when the people running the models know that is not true. Baum replied that he thinks the concept of a digital twin is unlikely to have much value for studying catastrophic risk because the systems are too poorly understood and too difficult to model.

Axtell noted that DoD often requires simulation models to assess the feasibility of military projects. Similar models play an important role in modern production processes, where the idea is to stress the system to see where it fails and learn where changes are needed. His guess was that by 2050 there will be enough data and computational power that nobody will do prototyping in hardware anymore, it will all be done computationally. His hope is that rare event modeling will also improve to the degree that it will be possible to simulate rare events and not have to live through them.

9

Concluding Remarks

To conclude the workshop, Christopher Barrett summarized the key points he heard over the 2 days. A salient theme that emerged within every workshop presentation was the idea that there are individual and tactical decisions that must be made inside of a world full of geopolitical complexity. Specifically, social systems, governance, organization structures, human involvement, and individual actions should be considered in tactical decision-making/ design of decision support technology. For example, Barrett noted his surprise at having heard of the geopolitical considerations involved with the deflection of asteroids. Barrett mentioned the importance of understanding how broader strategic considerations can constrain or define the value of tactical individual decisions.

Barrett also observed that data collection on rare events can be challenging because the systems of study and the sources of the rare events themselves are often co-evolving. An example of a co-evolving system is the human interaction associated with viral variants. When humans stress a virus (say by vaccines or therapeutics, which could restrict its transmission, and thus threaten its survival), it mutates into a new virus, which, in turn, changes the way humans behave in reaction to the variant. Thus, human behaviors co-evolve with the viral mutations. Barrett thus emphasized that collecting data to predict a world that is co-evolving with human responses needs deep consideration and focus.

In some cases, Barrett explained, research needs to adapt a "digital twin" style approach to research in order to get an idea of what the data should focus on and what should constitute the data in order to guide decisions and processes in this setting. Within this focus, there needs to be a determination of what are the appropriate data to measure—What are the appropriate tools and methods to obtain this information, and Whom will they ultimately support? It needs to align with processing information for decision-making and policymaking. Within this focus, there also needs to be included considerations of tactical and strategic organizations, enterprises, governments, societies, global populations, ecologies, economics, and the planet itself.

Barrett emphasized that the way we collect data should ultimately be informed by the type of deliverable that could benefit organizations and agencies like the DTRA and the Intelligence Community. This would be in the form of computational information technology, including AI and deep learning as well as advanced modeling and simulation approaches. This also would require a rethinking of how to convert current approaches in order to create platforms that would be most useful to such organizations. Such approaches would also need to embrace and aid analysts.

Barrett also highlighted the importance of the concept of "data commons," where data across different organizations could be shared and leveraged. As an example, Barrett suggested that there are relationships and connections across all various sub-communities associated with the analysis of weapons of mass destruction, their deterrence, their analysis, and the basic posturing and positioning with respect to them that could be leveraged.

Barrett concluded his remarks by noting that the importance of organizational evolution, especially in organizations engaged in intelligence preparation, is often underestimated and deserves more emphasis. Barrett listed the U.S. government's response to the pandemic as an example of normalizing the public institutional need to focus on pandemics and large-scale epidemics. Barrett noted that within this normalization there was a reorganization and an increased rate of government learning that happened as a reaction to COVID-19.

Appendixes

A

Statement of Task

The National Academies of Sciences, Engineering, and Medicine (the National Academies) will appoint a planning committee to organize a 2-day unclassified workshop focused on methods for anticipating rare events of major significance. Rare events are characterized by a very low probability of occurrence. Such events include anthropogenic hazards (e.g., weapons of mass destruction) and natural catastrophic events (e.g., pandemics).

The workshop will examine and moderate cross disciplinary discussions on rare event prediction methods, techniques, and best practices. Invited presentations will focus on:

1. Reviewing existing rare event prediction methods and models across academic disciplines and organizations;
2. Exploring opportunities and challenges in existing rare event prediction frameworks in order to define future anticipatory models.

The unclassified workshop will bring together the private sector and academia to (1) inform the Defense Threat Reduction Agency (DTRA) and the national security community of salient methods to anticipate rare events and (2) synthesize cross-disciplinary knowledge to define future prediction and anticipatory models. The planning committee will develop the workshop agenda, select and invite speakers and discussants, and moderate the discussions. An unclassified proceedings of the presentations and discussions at the workshop will be prepared by a designated rapporteur in accordance with institutional guidelines. These proceedings may be used to guide the development of more detailed National Academies activities on this topic.

B

Workshop Agenda

DAY 1: DECEMBER 17, 2021

Session 1 — Importance and Scope

10:30 AM **Introduction and Expectations of the Workshop**
Christopher Barrett, Committee Chair
University of Virginia Biocomplexity Institute

10:45 **Sponsor Remarks**
Theodore Plasse
Defense Threat Reduction Agency

Session 2 — Mathematical Foundations

11:00 Alon Orlitsky
University of California, San Diego

11:30 Break

Session 3 — Detection, Indications, and Warnings

11:45 Arvind Satyam
Pano AI

12:05 PM T. Charles Clancy
MITRE Labs

12:25 Elisabeth Paté-Cornell
Stanford University

APPENDIX B   *45*

12:45   Panel Discussion with Speakers 1–3
            Robert Schock, Moderator

1:20   Lunch

Session 4 — Planning, Forecasting, and Intelligence Preparation

2:15   Jeffrey J. Love
            U.S. Geological Survey

2:35   Nestor Alfonzo Santamaria
            Organisation for Economic Co-operation and Development

2:55   Madhav Marathe
            University of Virginia Biocomplexity Institute

3:15   Panel Discussion with Speakers 4–6
            Christopher Barrett, Moderator

3:50   Break

Session 5 — Fireside Chat

3:55   Madeleine Clare Elish
            Google Research

            Michele Wucker, Moderator

4:25   Day One Concluding Remarks
            Christopher Barrett, Committee Chair
            University of Virginia Biocomplexity Institute

4:30   Adjourn Day One

DAY 2: DECEMBER 21, 2021

Session 6 — Plenary

10:00 AM   Welcome and Introduction for Day 2
            Christopher Barrett, Committee Chair
            University of Virginia Biocomplexity Institute

10:05   Sponsor Remarks
            Theodore Plasse
            Defense Threat Reduction Agency

Session 7 — Fireside Chat

10:10　　Markus Gesmann
　　　　　Insurance Capital Markets Research

　　　　　Michele Wucker, Moderator

11:10　　Break

Session 8 — Multisource Information Fusion, Situation Assessment, and Course of Action Selection

11:25　　Alice Hill
　　　　　Council on Foreign Relations

11:45　　Delores Knipp
　　　　　University of Colorado Boulder

12:05 PM　John Organek
　　　　　Electric Infrastructure Security Council

12:25　　Panel Discussion with Speakers 7–9
　　　　　Vicki Bier, Moderator

1:00　　 Lunch

Session 9 — Active Prevention and Deterrence

1:50　　 Terik Daly
　　　　　Johns Hopkins University Applied Physics Laboratory

2:10　　 Seth Baum
　　　　　Global Catastrophic Risk Institute

2:30　　 Robert Axtell
　　　　　George Mason University

2:50　　 Panel Discussion with Speakers 10-12
　　　　　Justin Kasper, Moderator

3:25　　 Concluding Remarks
　　　　　Christopher Barrett, Committee Chair
　　　　　University of Virginia Biocomplexity Institute

3:35　　 Adjourn Workshop

C

Planning Committee Biographies

CHRISTOPHER L. BARRETT, *Chair*, is an Endowed Distinguished Professor in Biocomplexity, the founding executive director of the Biocomplexity Institute, and a professor of the Department of Computer Science at the University of Virginia. Over the past 35 years, Barrett has conceived, founded, and led interdisciplinary complex systems research projects and organizations, established national and international technology programs, and co-founded organizations for federal agencies, including the Department of Defense (DoD), the Department of Energy, the Department of Homeland Security, and the Department of Transportation. Barrett received the 2012–2013 Jubilee Professorship in Computer Science and Engineering at Chalmers University in Sweden and is a member of the 2010 Royal Colloquium for the King of Sweden. He was a distinguished international professor at the Royal Institute of Technology in Stockholm. He has received Distinguished Research, Service, Advisory, and Security Awards from the U.S. Navy, Los Alamos National Laboratory, and the Alliance for Transportation Research. He has served as an adviser to U.S. government agencies, the Commonwealth of Virginia, the European Commission, and others. He is the author and co-author of more than 100 peer-reviewed papers and presentations. He holds 7 patents and has 10 pending. Barrett holds a Ph.D. in bioinformation systems/engineering science and an M.S. in engineering science from the California Institute of Technology and a U.S. Navy Aerospace Experimental Psychology, Medical Service Corps post Ph.D. certification.

DAVID ALDOUS is professor emeritus at the Department of Statistics, University of California (UC), Berkeley. Previously he was the chair (1997–1999), professor (1986–2018), associate professor (1982–1986), and assistant professor (1979–1982) at the Department of Statistics, UC Berkeley. Aldous is a member of the National Academy of Sciences and has received numerous awards, including the Brouwer Medal (2020), American Mathematical Society fellow (2012), and Docteur Honoris Causa de l'Universite de Provence (2011). Aldous received a B.A. and a Ph.D. in mathematics from Cambridge University in 1973 and 1977, respectively.

VICKI M. BIER is professor emerita in the Department of Industrial and Systems Engineering and the Department of Engineering Physics at the University of Wisconsin–Madison, where she directed the Center for Human Performance and Risk Analysis (formerly the Center for Human Performance in Complex Systems) from 1995 to 2021. She was recently appointed to the Advisory Committee on Reactor Safeguards of the U.S. Nuclear Regulatory Commission. She has more than 40 years of experience in risk analysis for the nuclear power, chemical, petrochemical, and aerospace industries, as well as homeland security and critical-infrastructure protection. Bier's recent research has focused on applications of risk analysis and related methods to problems of security, critical infrastructure protection, and emergency management. Bier received the Women's Achievement Award from the American Nuclear Society in 1993, and was elected a fellow of the Society for Risk Analysis in 1996, from which she received the Distinguished Achievement Award in 2007. She is also a past president of the Decision Analysis Society, and editor in chief of the society's flagship journal, *Decision Analysis*. She has participated in panels, committees, and subcommittees of the National Academies of Sciences, Engineering, and Medicine dealing with radioactive waste management and a committee to review the Department of Homeland Security's approach to risk analysis, and served on the Board on Mathematical Sciences and Analytics from 2014 to 2016. She received a Ph.D. in operations research from the Massachusetts Institute of Technology in 1983, and a B.S. in mathematical sciences from Stanford University in 1976.

DAN FUKUSHIMA is a director and futurist at Toffler Associates, the firm founded by noted futurist Alvin Toffler. For more than 30 years, he has been helping organizations recognize, prepare for, and take advantage of how the future may unfold. His career is a collection of diverse experiences linked by the common thread of disruption. Starting in the airline industry as deregulation, market innovation and new technology took hold, he had a first-hand view that has shaped his perspective on analyzing the future. He further honed his insightful, creative, and pragmatic approach to futures and foresight in work within the financial services, retail, and consumer products industries during disruptive transformations. In recent work across DoD, Fukushima has applied this approach to planning the future of Army installations, analyzing the research and manufacturing landscape for DoD science and technology organizations, preparing for climate impacts to continental U.S. installations, and addressing the future of talent for a military research laboratory. His goal is to help leaders understand how future shifts impact current decisions and anticipate and plan for unique events and disruptive scenarios through analysis and imagination. He is a graduate of the Georgia Institute of Technology.

JUSTIN C. KASPER is the deputy chief technology officer for BWX Technologies (BWXT), which is the sole manufacturer of nuclear reactors for the U.S. Navy. He maintains a fractional appointment as professor in the University of Michigan Department of Climate and Space Sciences and Engineering and was previously a Smithsonian Institution civil servant. Kasper is an experimental physicist by training, with experience developing electromagnetic and particle sensors and systems for the exploration of space and operation in extreme environments. He is the principal investigator of the SWEAP Investigation on Parker Solar Probe and of the six-spacecraft SunRISE Explorer mission. At BWXT his responsibilities include execution of company research and development efforts, management of intellectual property, and the identification of new products and technologies. He has received the Presidential Early Career Award for Scientists and Engineers (2010), the Henry Russel Award (2018), and numerous NASA awards and is a member of the American Geophysical Union and the American Physical Society. He received his A.B. in physics from the University of Chicago and Ph.D. in physics from the Massachusetts Institute of Technology. He served on the Steering Committee of the 2013 Decadal Surface in Solar and Space Physics and is a member of the Intelligence Science and Technology Experts Group.

CATO T. LAURENCIN is a designated university professor at the University of Connecticut, one of only two currently at the school. He earned his B.S.E. in chemical engineering from Princeton University, his M.D., magna cum laude, from the Harvard Medical School, and his Ph.D. in biochemical engineering/biotechnology from the Massachusetts Institute of Technology. Laurencin's life and career have been rooted in his passion for service to our nation. He has been a scholar in discussing issues involving health disparities and social justice, publishing the first peer-reviewed article on COVID-19 and Black Americans. His paper "Medical Surprise Anticipation and Recognition Capability: A New Concept for Better Health Care" presaged our need to prepare for unexpected medical events such as COVID-19. He has participated in National Academies' activities surrounding anthrax (*Review of the Scientific Approaches Used During the FBI's Investigation of the 2001 Anthrax Letters*) and the U.S. military's capability for surprise (*Responding to Capability Surprise Strategy for U.S. Naval Forces* in 2013). In addition, Laurencin is the founder of the field of regenerative engineering. He is the first surgeon in history elected to the National Academy of Sciences, the National Academy of Engineering, the National Academy of Medicine,

APPENDIX C

the National Academy of Inventors, and the American Academy of Arts & Sciences. He has singular distinctions. In science, he received the Philip Hauge Abelson Prize from the American Association for the Advancement of Science "for signal contributions to the advancement of science in the United States." In engineering, he received the Simon Ramo Founders Award from the National Academy of Engineering, its oldest/highest award. In medicine, he received the Walsh McDermott Medal from the National Academy of Medicine, one its oldest/highest awards, and in technology he received the National Medal of Technology and Innovation, America's highest honor for technological achievement awarded by the President of the United States.

ALON ORLITSKY graduated from Stanford University with a Ph.D. in electrical engineering. He is currently a professor of electrical and computer engineering and computer science and engineering at UC San Diego where he holds the Qualcomm Chair in Information Theory and Its Applications. He was selected for membership on this committee for his work on learning from scarce data and on predicting rare and even unseen events, which received several paper awards from the *IEEE Transactions on Information Theory* and the NeurIPS and International Conference on Machine Learning conferences.

ROBERT N. SCHOCK is a senior fellow at the Center for Global Security Research at Lawrence Livermore National Laboratory. He is also the co-chair of the Energy and the Catastrophic Risk Permanent Monitoring Panels for the World Federation of Scientists, and a senior adviser and the former director of studies for the World Energy Council in London. He was a coordinating lead author (Energy Sources) for the Fourth Assessment Report of the Intergovernmental Panel on Climate Change. He was a lead author on the 2012 Global Energy Assessment. For 34 years at Lawrence Livermore National Laboratory, he held a number of positions up to and including associate director in which he initiated or was responsible for programs in advanced energy technologies including magnetic fusion, hydrogen fuels, geothermal, in-situ coal gasification, oil shale retorting, environmental restoration and nuclear waste management, and energy policy analysis. He was a delegate to the U.S.–Russian bilateral negotiations on nuclear nonproliferation (1999–2000) and worked on verification of the Agreed Framework with North Korea (2001). Schock has served on the editorial boards of five scientific journals and on national scientific panels for the U.S. National Research Council, the Department of Energy, and the National Science Foundation. He was a Senior Fulbright Fellow in Germany and a visiting fellow at the Australian National University. He is an author or co-author of more than 150 scientific and technical papers. He holds a B.S. in geology from Colorado College, an M.S. in geochemistry from Rensselaer Polytechnic Institute, and a Ph.D. in geophysics also from Rensselaer.

MICHELE WUCKER is the founder and chief executive officer of the Chicago-based strategy firm Gray Rhino & Company (www.thegrayrhino.com). She coined the term *gray rhino* to draw attention to the need to better respond to obvious, highly probable risks. Decision makers are surprisingly likely—though not condemned—to neglect, downplay, or outright ignore these gray rhino dangers despite—indeed, often because of—their size and likelihood. The timely metaphor and supporting framework have moved markets, shaped financial policies, and made headlines around the world, especially as a frame for the ignored warnings that led to the COVID-19 pandemic. Wucker's 2019 TED Talk has attracted more than 2 million views. She is the author of four books, including the global best-seller *The Gray Rhino: How to Recognize and Act on the Obvious Dangers We Ignore* (2016); and *You Are What You Risk: The New Art and Science of Navigating an Uncertain World* (2021). Drawing on three decades of experience in financial media and think tank management, turnarounds, and economic policy analysis, Wucker speaks regularly to high-level global audiences on risk management, macro strategy, and decision-making; and writes for and is quoted often in leading media. She holds a B.A. from Rice University and a master's degree from Columbia University's School of International and Public Affairs. She has been recognized as a Young Global Leader of the World Economic Forum and a Guggenheim Fellow, among other honors.

D

Speaker Biographies

ROBERT AXTELL is a professor of computational social science at George Mason University, external faculty fellow at the Santa Fe Institute, and is presently visiting professor at the Sloan School of Management at the Massachusetts Institute of Technology (MIT). He works at the intersection of the computational, economic, and behavioral sciences. Axtell's research group combines agent-based computing with micro-data to build large-scale models having high verisimilitude with the real world. He has worked on a variety of policy issues, from housing to fisheries, behavioral aspects of retirement, and national defense. His research has been published in leading journals like *Science* and the *Proceedings of the National Academy of Sciences*, as well in field journals (e.g., *American Economic Review, The Economic Journal, Sustainability Science*) and in computer science conference proceedings (e.g., *Autonomous Agents and Multiagent Systems*). His work has been covered by many newspapers (e.g., *The Wall Street Journal, The Washington Post, Los Angeles Times*) and magazines (e.g., *Technology Review, Wired, New Scientist*). He is the co-author (with J.M. Epstein) of *Growing Artificial Societies: Social Science from the Bottom Up*, an early statement of the agent-based research program applied to questions in the social sciences. Axtell spent nearly 15 years at the Brookings Institution, lastly as senior fellow in the Economics Studies and Governance Studies Programs. For the past 15 years, he has taught at George Mason University, serving most of that time as chair of the Department of Computational Social Science while teaching agent-based modeling at both the undergraduate and graduate levels. He has been a visiting professor at the University of Oxford (Institute for New Economic Thinking and Hertford College) and the Mellon Visiting Distinguished Professor at Middlebury College.

CHRISTOPHER L. BARRETT is an Endowed Distinguished Professor in Biocomplexity, the founding executive director of the Biocomplexity Institute, and a professor of the Department of Computer Science at the University of Virginia. Over the past 35 years, Barrett has conceived, founded, and led interdisciplinary complex systems research projects and organizations, established national and international technology programs, and co-founded organizations for federal agencies, including the Department of Defense (DoD), the Department of Energy, the Department of Homeland Security, and the Department of Transportation. Barrett received the 2012–2013 Jubilee Professorship in Computer Science and Engineering at Chalmers University in Sweden and is a member of the 2010 Royal Colloquium for the King of Sweden. He was a distinguished international professor at the Royal Institute of Technology in Stockholm. He has received Distinguished Research, Service, Advisory, and Security Awards from the U.S. Navy, Los Alamos National Laboratory, and the Alliance for Transportation Research. He has served as an adviser to U.S. government agencies, the Commonwealth of Virginia, the European Commission, and others.

He is the author and co-author of more than 100 peer-reviewed papers and presentations. He holds 7 patents and has 10 pending. Barrett holds a Ph.D. in bioinformation systems/engineering science and an M.S. in engineering science from the California Institute of Technology and a U.S. Navy Aerospace Experimental Psychology, Medical Service Corps post Ph.D. certification.

SETH D. BAUM is the co-founder and executive director of the Global Catastrophic Risk Institute, a nonprofit and nonpartisan think tank. He is also a research affiliate of the Centre for the Study of Existential Risk at the University of Cambridge and an associate editor of the journal *Science & Engineering Ethics*. He leads an interdisciplinary research agenda of risk, ethics, and policy analysis of catastrophic risks, focusing primarily on artificial intelligence and nuclear war. Baum received degrees in optics, applied mathematics, and electrical engineering before completing a Ph.D. in geography from Pennsylvania State University and a postdoctoral fellowship in psychology at Columbia University.

T. CHARLES CLANCY is a senior vice president and general manager of MITRE Labs and chief futurist at MITRE. He is responsible for sparking innovative disruption, accelerating risk-taking and discovery, and delivering real-time technology capabilities and execution through the company's laboratories, solution platforms, and MITRE fellows program. He leads technical innovation to anticipate and meet the future demands of government sponsors and industry and academic partners. Clancy is an internationally recognized expert on topics at the intersection of wireless, cybersecurity, and artificial intelligence. Before joining MITRE in 2019 as the vice president for intelligence programs, Clancy served as the Bradley Distinguished Professor in Cybersecurity at Virginia Tech and the executive director at the Hume Center for National Security and Technology. There, he led Virginia Tech's research and experiential learning programs in defense and intelligence. He started his career at the National Security Agency, filling a variety of research, engineering, and operations roles, with a focus on wireless communications. He has co-authored more than 250 patents and academic publications, as well as 6 books. He co-founded several venture-backed security startup companies that apply commercial innovation to national security challenges. Clancy is an Institute of Electrical and Electronics Engineers (IEEE) fellow and sits on the AFCEA International board of directors' executive committee, the AFCEA Intelligence Committee, the Intelligence and National Security Alliance advisory committee, the Systems Engineering Research Center advisory board, the Alliance for Telecommunications Industry Solutions Next G Alliance, and the Center for New American Security Task Force on Artificial Intelligence and National Security. He also serves on advisory boards at Howard University, Norfolk State University, North Carolina A&T State University, and Virginia Tech. In 2021, *WashingtonExec* magazine named Clancy one of the nation's Top Climate Executives to Watch. Clancy holds a bachelor's degree in computer engineering from the Rose-Hulman Institute of Technology, a master's degree in electrical engineering from the University of Illinois at Urbana-Champaign, and a doctorate in computer science from the University of Maryland, College Park.

TERIK DALY is a senior staff scientist at the Johns Hopkins University Applied Physics Laboratory. He works on NASA missions that study near-Earth asteroids, including the OSIRIS-REx mission that will return an asteroid sample to Earth in 2023. He is the deputy instrument scientist for the Double Asteroid Redirection Test, which is the nation's first planetary defense test mission and launched in November 2021. He also contributes to efforts to defend Earth against the hazards posed by asteroids and comets as part of the organizing committees for the biannual Planetary Defense Conference and tabletop exercises. Daly is the principal investigator for multiple NASA-funded grants that address pressing problems in planetary science.

MADELEINE CLARE ELISH is a cultural anthropologist whose work examines the social impacts of artificial intelligence (AI) and automation on society. She joined Google as a senior research scientist and currently leads the Responsible AI team for Cloud AI. Previously, she co-founded and led the AI on the Ground Initiative at the Data and Society Research Institute, which uses social science research to inform future design, use, and governance of data-driven systems. She also serves on the executive committee of the Association for Computing Machinery (ACM) Fairness and Accountability in Machine Learning computer science conference, after having served as conference general co-chair in 2021. She has conducted field work across varied industries and communities, ranging from the Air Force, the driverless car industry, and commercial aviation to precision agriculture and emergency health care. Her research has been published and cited in scholarly journals as well as publications, including *The New York Times*, *Wired*, *The Guardian*, *MIT Tech Review*, *Vice*, and *USA Today*. She holds a Ph.D. in anthropology from Columbia University and an S.M. in comparative media studies from MIT.

MARKUS GERMANN is the co-founder of Insurance Capital Markets Research. A research house that provides quantitative research on the global specialty (re)insurance industry for insurance carriers, intermediaries, and investors. Germann has spent the past 18 years in the London insurance and capital markets, heading up the analysis function at Lloyd's of London for 8 years. He is a mathematician by background and has carried out research on how Bayesian analysis and probabilistic programming can be applied in insurance to assess risk. Furthermore, Germann is the co-founder of the Insurance Data Science conference series and the London Bayesian Mixer meet-ups.

ALICE HILL is the David M. Rubenstein Senior Fellow for Energy and the Environment at the Council on Foreign Relations (CFR). Her work at CFR focuses on the risks, consequences, and responses associated with climate change. Hill previously served as the special assistant to President Barack Obama and the senior director for resilience policy on the National Security Council staff where she led the development of national policy to build resilience to catastrophic risks, including climate change and biological threats. Prior to this, Hill served as the senior counselor to the secretary of the Department of Homeland Security (DHS), in which she led the formulation of DHS's first-ever climate adaptation plan and the development of strategic plans regarding catastrophic biological and chemical threats, including pandemics. Earlier in her career, she was a supervising judge on both the Los Angeles Municipal and Superior Courts as well as a federal prosecutor and chief of the white-collar crime unit at the United States Attorney's Office in Los Angeles, California. Oxford University Press published her co-authored book, *Building a Resilient Tomorrow*, in 2019. She currently serves on the boards of the Environmental Defense Fund and Munich Re Group's U.S.-based companies. In 2020, Yale University and the Op-Ed Project awarded her the Public Voices Fellowship on the Climate Crisis. Hill's new book, *The Fight for Climate After COVID-19*, was published in September 2021.

DELORES KNIPP is a research professor at the Smead Aerospace Engineering Sciences Department at the University of Colorado Boulder (CU Boulder). She earned a Ph.D. in atmospheric and space physics from the University of California, Los Angeles, in 1989. Her career spans more than 30 years as an active-duty Air Force Officer and civilian professor at the U.S. Air Force Academy where she taught physics, meteorology, and astronomy, followed by more than a decade of teaching and research at CU Boulder. During that time, she wrote the first space weather textbook for upper division undergraduates titled "Understanding Space Weather and the Physics Behind It." In 2005–2006, she served on National Space Weather Program Assessment Committee; in 2015–2016 she served on the National Science Foundation Portfolio Review Committee of the Geospace Section, Division of Atmospheric and Geospace Sciences. From 2014 to 2019, Knipp was the editor in chief for the American Geophysical Union's (AGU's) *Space Weather Journal*. During that time, Knipp delivered the 2017 Coupling Energetics and Dynamics of Atmospheric Regions (CEDAR) Prize lecture, "Nitric Oxide: How the Thermosphere 'Fights Back' During Intense Storms." In 2019, she was a member Next Step Space Weather Benchmarks Working Group and co-convened the AGU Chapman Conference on Forecasting Space Weather Including Extremes. Most recently, she has served as the 2019–2021 chair of the Coupling Energetic & Dynamics of Atmospheric Regions (CEDAR) Science Steering Committee. In 2019, she joined the ranks of fellows at the American Meteorological Society. Later that year, she was awarded the 2019 International Marcel Nicolet Medal for Space Weather and Space Climate and delivered the Michael J. Buonsanto 20th Annual Memorial Lecture at MIT Haystack Observatory. Knipp's research focuses on the space environment and the atmospheric and solar events that disturb it. She works with students to investigate methods for (1) specifying satellite drag; (2) describing how structures on the Sun produce disturbances in near-Earth space; (3) improving scientific use of space environment measurements from DoD, NASA, and international space missions; (4) inter-comparing measurements from research and commercial satellites with an eye toward making broader use of commercial satellite "housekeeping" data to monitor environmental conditions in near-

Earth space; (5) describing the effects of extreme space weather at Earth; and (6) developing educational material related to space weather. She also studies historical space weather events to understand the impacts these events have had on society and the U.S. military. She and her group are also working to prepare historical space weather datasets for machine learning extreme-event detection.

JEFFREY J. LOVE has an A.B. in physics from the University of California, Berkeley, and a Ph.D. in geophysics from Harvard University. After receiving his doctorate in 1993, Love worked at the University of Leeds, England, the Atomic Energy Commission, France, and the Scripps Institution for Oceanography, La Jolla, California. In 2001, he was hired by the U.S. Geological Survey (USGS) as a research geophysicist, and he is presently the USGS Adviser for Geomagnetic Research. Love works in collaboration with colleagues on three subjects: (1) using geomagnetic monitoring data and magnetotelluric survey data to evaluate geoelectric hazards of concern to the electric-power grid industry, (2) statistical analysis of the rare occurrences of intense magnetic storms, and (3) analysis of historical records of past space-weather events and their impacts. Love also works to coordinate USGS projects with other government agencies through the Space Weather Operations Research and Mitigation (SWORM) working group of the National Science and Technology Council (NSTC).

MADHAV MARATHE is a Distinguished Professor in Biocomplexity, the division director of the Networks, Simulation Science and Advanced Computing Division at the Biocomplexity Institute and Initiative, and a professor in the Department of Computer Science at the University of Virginia (UVA). His research interests are in network science, computational epidemiology, AI, foundations of computing, socially coupled system science, and high performance computing. Over the past 25 years, he and his colleagues have developed scalable computational methods to study the social, economic, and health impacts of large-scale natural and human initiated disasters. The tools and methods have been used in more than 50 case studies to inform and assess various policy questions pertaining to planning and response in the event of such disasters. Before joining UVA, he held positions at Virginia Tech, Los Alamos National Laboratory, and was the inaugural George Michael Fellow at the Lawrence Livermore National Laboratory. He is a fellow of the American Association for the Advancement of Science (AAAS), the Society for Industrial and Applied Mathematics, the ACM, and the IEEE.

JOHN ORGANEK is a senior program developer for more than 30 years, with a focus on leading the transformation of national-level organizations to better align with their value proposition through the challenging technical and human change efforts demanded: strategic planning, enterprise architecture, business process management, and infrastructure investment portfolio management. He was an officer in the U.S. Army Corps of Engineers for more than 23 years, serving in an eclectic portfolio of leadership and staff roles including combat command, chief of engineer planning, Combined Forces Command (Republic of Korea), the Army staff, and Office of the Secretary (Army). Functional specialties include combat engineering, construction, information technology, and operations research. For 6 years, he was the Senior Executive Service chief architect for Army Business Systems supporting U.S. Army business transformation. He applied extensive system-of-systems education in water resources, economics, and regional planning to large-scale business transformation efforts for the U.S. Army, the Republic of Korea, the NASDAQ Stock Market, and the Federal Reserve.

ALON ORLITSKY graduated from Stanford University with a Ph.D. in electrical engineering. He is currently a professor of electrical and computer engineering and computer science and engineering at UC San Diego where he holds the Qualcomm Chair in Information Theory and Its Applications. He was selected for membership on this committee for his work on learning from scarce data and on predicting rare and even unseen events, which received several paper awards from the *IEEE Transactions on Information Theory* and the NeurIPS and International Conference on Machine Learning conferences.

M. ELISABETH PATÉ-CORNELL is the Burt and Deedee McMurtry Professor and chair of the Department of Management Science and Engineering at Stanford University. Her specialty is engineering risk analysis with application to complex systems (space, medical). Her research has focused on explicit consideration of human and organizational factors in the analysis of failure risks, and recently on the use of game theory in risk analysis. Applications in the past few years have included counter-terrorism and nuclear counter-proliferation problems. She is a member of several boards, including Aerospace, Draper, and InQtel. She was a member of the President's Foreign Intelligence Advisory Board until December 2008. She received a Ph.D. in engineering economic systems from Stanford University. Paté-Cornell was elected to the National Academy of Engineering in 1995.

NESTOR ALFONZO SANTAMARIA is an expert in adaptation and disaster risk management and currently serves as a senior adviser on risk governance for the Organisation for Economic Co-operation and Development working for the Governance Reviews and Partnerships Division, within the Public Governance Directorate. Prior to his current position, he worked on resilience and disaster management policy in several UK ministries and for the government of London's Financial District (the City of London). Santamaria has also advised on disaster management issues for the European Union, various United Nations agencies, the World Bank, and the Inter-American Development Bank. In Latin America, he has worked on political violence prevention and peacebuilding initiatives, electoral observation, human rights promotion, and support to refugees/internally displaced persons.

ARVAND SATYAM is the chief commercial officer of Pano, a purpose-driven business to address climate change–related disasters and infrastructure resilience using Internet of Things (IoT) and artificial intelligence solutions, and a venture partner at Ozone Ventures. Previously, managing director, Global Public Sector at Cisco, he led growth initiatives for $13 billion public-sector business including critical infrastructure, cybersecurity strategy for state and national governments, and public–private partnerships with multinational institutions. Formerly, Satyam led telco service provider sales, strategic partnerships, and venture investments for Cisco's IoT & Smart City businesses. He is an investor and adviser to several companies; on the advisory board of the startups, World Sensing, EQITII and Urbanise, and a member of the Governor of Illinois's technology advisory board. Passionate about connecting technology to human outcomes he is an academy judge for the $1M Varkey Foundation Global Teacher Prize. He has contributed to articles for *The Wall Street Journal, Bloomberg Finance, The Atlantic, The New York Times, Fortune, Harvard Business School Alumni Magazine,* and *L'Atelier.* Satyam was named a Young Global Leader by the World Economic Forum in 2018 and a Young Leader by World Cities Summit in 2016. He holds a holds a bachelor's degree in computer engineering and a master's degree in finance from the University of New South Wales and is an alumnus of Harvard Business School. During his studies at the Kenan-Flagler Business School of the University of North Carolina he was an Adams advisor.